JUST A
THOUGHT

Creating the Life You Deserve
from the Inside Out

DAVID A. VOLPE

Cover/Interior Design by: Ida Fia Sveningsson.
Find her at www.idafiasveningsson.se.

ACKNOWLEDGEMENTS

A special Thank You

To my parents, my sister, and to you, the reader.

CONTENTS

PART THREE: MINDFUL HAPPPINESS

PART FOUR: CONNECT

PART FIVE: LIVE

WHAT'S IN IT FOR YOU?

Nothing, other than what you choose to take away. The thoughts that occur in your mind indeed will not only impact your life, but shape the very reality of it. Your mindset alone will either create or diminish your potential to design the life of your dreams. Before continuing, I need you to understand and sign this contract with yourself below:

1. I am capable of anything, absolutely anything I set my mind to.
2. I do deserve to achieve my dreams.
3. My life and how I live it is up to me and only me.
4. Happiness, success, and the best life imaginable are meant for me.
5. I was born for greatness.
6. I am unique, special and beautiful, and there is no one in the world like me.
7. I believe that every single word I have just read is true.

SIGN HERE:

CONGRATULATIONS.

WELCOME TO THE REST OF YOUR LIFE.

INTRODUCTION

Your thoughts are the foundation to the creation of your life. Reality is shaped from the inside out. Take control of your thoughts and destiny. The journey to a beautiful life begins within you, and travels outward from your thoughts, intentions, actions, and reactions into to the world around you.

Your life is yours to create the masterpiece you see in your dreams. Take control of your fate by harnessing the power in your mind and then shifting toward your greatest desires with burning purpose and vigorous positivity.

Above all, this book is a reminder to live and love life to the fullest of your ability. You have the chance to discover a clear sense of who you are, how to possess your heart's most burning desire, and mindfully create the happiness within the life you deserve. This was written for you and only you. Its purpose is to develop your mind and shift your consciousness to life's possibilities.

No matter who is reading this; my goal is to connect with you. That is what life is all about: Connection. A deep and conscious connection to yourself, others, your desires, and to what surrounds you is what I aim to provoke from within you. Let this be your guide to what's inside.

This book has found its way into your hands at this very moment in your life for a reason. It's your job to find out why. Everything you are about to read was meant to enhance your life and bring you closer to making it into all it can be.

Know that every word past this point is a suggestion, a guide, and a simple spark to ignite your best life starting now. I'm not telling you what to do or how to live; it's simply *Just a Thought*. What you choose to do next is up to you.

> "*I can't teach you anything, I can only make you think.*"
>
> – SOCRATES

Before continuing, please do these 4 things: Open your mind, Open your Heart, Deeply inhale, Deeply Exhale.

Enjoy!

SECTION ONE
SUCCEED

CHAPTER 1

WHAT'S YOUR WHY?

"It's the possibility of having a dream come true is what makes life interesting."

– PAULO COELHO

It's a spark that starts a fire—just one thought—a single dream that possesses the potential to change everything. The incredible fact that you can dream it makes it possible to achieve. Breathing life into a single word...possibility. Just like that, your life can change. The mind is limitless, and the possibilities are endless. It starts with just a single thought. It originates with a dream. It begins with your WHY.

WHAT DO YOU FEEL EVERY MORNING?

Following the first light that enters your pupils every morning, what do you feel about coming events in your day? Do you rise and prepare for a day that causes you to spring you from bed as if it's on fire at the very thought of it? Or, do you instead prepare for one that binds you to it, as sanctuary from your life outside of its comforting embrace? Most importantly, are you waking up in a world in which you are doing something you love? Success isn't what creates happiness; it's quite the opposite, in fact. Happiness is found within doing what you love, and letting that pave the way to a desired end. Purpose is a powerful propellant. It is the very gas that fuels the engine in your life. Do you know it? Is it guiding you?

The reason for doing something is just as or more important than the act of actually doing it. Finding the fire that burns your desire is the precursor to your obsession to succeed in anything. You will never find happiness on a path that leads to somewhere you never wanted to go in the first place. Setting goals that will bring you happiness by embarking on the journey itself will satisfy you more than doing something just for the sake of doing it. Having passion and a mindset to a strong enough purpose shall never taste defeat.

Anything we do is anchored by desire and the root of it, the **why** behind the **what**. Recognize this, and your path will become visible and powerfully purposeful. Indulge your imagination. That's the very first step in attracting anything of worth into your life. We're so hard on our imagination. Spoil it; let your mind shed light on what makes you excited. There's such beauty in the extraordinary simplicity of the word **excitement**. Such a word could set fire to water. What once was a dream can now be a reality, in light of the word, and can be the way to get you there.

HOW BADLY DO YOU WANT IT?

The things in which we tend to place the most value are ironically not actual things. They're abstract and are heavily weighted words such as passion, dreams, happiness, love, core values, relationships, and legacy. You must want it so bad that it becomes an obsession. Your sun needs to rise and set with your burning desire to get what makes your heart beat within your chest. Every thought needs to influence the next. Possessing a desire is like playing chess, in which you must think two or three moves ahead of your current intention. If this current action does not have a relationship to the next one, then it is deemed unnecessary in pursuit of your goal. It's as simple as that. Many people have a hard time starting or continuing, because they don't have a strong enough why. If your vision is clear and you act with purpose in alignment with your why, then everything will fall into place.

Conceptualizing your Why:

1. Why do you want this over everything else?
2. What is the origin of this desire?
3. What excites you?
4. What gets you out of bed in the morning?
5. What adds value to your life?
6. What will achieving this desire mean to you?
7. Are you creating your life or is it being created for you?

IT'S TIME

It's time to stop swimming upstream. Create your own current and be swept away by its intensity with your mind at ease, because you know its direction and destination. Positive- and purpose-driven thoughts turned actions guide you into the jet stream of success. Whatever you desire shall be yours in time when sprouted from the right Why.

It's time to eliminate fear of the unknown. Once you believe in the reason for why you're doing something, then fear instantly fades in its wake. You will begin to realize that there is no more fear of failure, because your purpose is strong enough and the choice to turn back has vanished. You WILL find a way.

"If something burns your soul with purpose and desire, it's your duty to be reduced to ashes by it. Any other form of existence will be yet another dull book in the library of life."

– CHARLES BUKOWSKI

What burns your soul? What are your deepest desires? Are you listening to what calls for you? In a book in which you're both the author and the main character, would you read it? Will the same desires you have today be reflected in your main characters' actions? Or, will the fire turn to embers and ash, once burning white hot, now only to leave a trail of smoke that reads of a plot evoking emotions of regret and loss? The story is yours and a new chapter starts now. It's time.

CHALLENGE

Right now! Write down (in your text drafts or on paper) a list of goals that excite you, anything and everything that comes to mind. Then, next to that list, write down why you want it. Finally, prioritize that list starting with "1" ranking each goal, predicated on how strong your reason for doing it is.

HINT

Your results should compare to that of an iceberg ranging from deep, life-changing desires to superficial instant gratifications with the purpose for them to align in importance to you.

CHAPTER 2

KNOW YOURSELF

"You were born an original, don't die a copy"

–JOHN MASON

There is no stronger compass in life guiding you in the direction of your deepest desires than self-actualization. Never given, only earned through trial and error, triumph, defeat, and most importantly taking that very first step in the right direction. Your journey begins with a single thought, turned feeling, accompanied by massive action. If you wait to know yourself before starting anything, you will forever be where you are right now. Think about any destination; there is a gap between you and it, where you are and where you wish to be. That gap is where you will discover yourself. It's less about getting there, and rather, who you become on the way.

HOW DOES ONE BECOME SELF-AWARE?

I don't know. I don't possess the answer, you do. It's not so much an answer rather than an adventure. The power of becoming self-aware will make all the difference in your life moving forward, living from a truly authentic place. It allows you to live life with joy and confidence when derived from authenticity. No one can tell you how to achieve it. There's no map to a treasure such as this. However, you can start by asking yourself the right questions in light of what drives you from within. The greatest wisdom is to understand your invisible self, rather than polishing your public appearance. What does that person want? What drives what's deep beneath your skin? What is seen on the outside is for everyone else, and what you know about yourself on the inside is what you need to be bringing into the light. What am I good at? What am I bad at? What do I like? What are my dislikes? Dig deep and ask yourself, who do I want to be? Not what, but who. Put your ear to your heart and act accordingly.

We tend to hide behind a veil of excuses and actions contrary to our authentic selves. The truer you are with expressing your feelings, desires, and needs, the less you'll need to think about how thick that veil is. That's the ultimate goal after all, right? Know yourself and becoming comfortable enough to live as that person, being guided by your choices and habits that get you to that place of self-actualization.

> "Knowing others is wisdom, knowing yourself is enlightenment"

– LAU-TZU

NEVER...

1. Never be ashamed of who you are. You must find and embrace your identity. Never abandon it. You are unique and destined for greatness in your life, and it's up to you to unlock your potential.

---

2. Never settle for anything less than exactly what you want. To settle means to accept mediocrity or something that's "good enough," and that's not who you are. Know yourself and let others follow your lead.

3. Never find yourself among the herd unless you wish to be lost. Avoid aimless wandering, adopting the qualities of others in sad attempts to create false identities in place of the one you are gifted with, but fail to recognize the beauty of. I'll tell you a secret you may or may not believe: you are good enough and deserve nothing less than exactly what you want out of your life. No exceptions. Find yourself and never let go.

4. Never give energy to what conjures negative emotions. It only produces negativity inside and out, feeding false beliefs that you're not good enough. Put yourself in positions where your strengths are highlighted, thus creating confidence and a genuine interest to explore that side of yourself, while allowing your personality to shine. Seek challenges, but never defeat yourself.

IDENTITY-SHAPING CHOICES

Start making conscious choices that point you in the right direction. To truly live a successful and happy life, your decisions must reflect your true authentic nature in accordance with who you are.

RIGHT PATH...

1. Trust your gut. Never ignore your intuition. You unconsciously know more than you'll ever be aware of.
2. The right choice is harder than the wrong one. What's right for you often requires sacrifice, abandoning your comfort zone, and appeasing others.

3. Accept, don't suppress your desires. Recognize, accept, and explore what stirs your curiosity.

4. Frightening. If it scares you, then do it. Find out who you are in the face of fear.

5. It may hurt you now, but help you later. Focus on what your future self will thank you for.

Notice a pattern? We all know what we really want and what we know we should do, but it starts getting lost in the noise and scrutiny of the world. The hardest choices to make are usually the right ones. Listen to your inner voice of encouragement and ignore the one who intend only to doubt and deter you from who you are.

WRONG PATH...

1. Ignoring your gut.
2. Doing it because it's easier.
3. Making someone else happy at the expense of your own.
4. Making excuses for things in your life instead of changing them.
5. Coping with the bad to hold onto the good.
6. Immediately regretting the moment you knew you could change your life, but didn't.

Things tend to snowball over time if you're not honest with yourself. Think about your favorite color, you favorite movie, or favorite anything for that matter. Now think about each of those things against something less desirable to you. Then, you're asked "This or That?" Obviously, without hesitation, you're going to pick all your favorite things. The same analogy can be applied to any choice in our life. So when life presents the options of "this or that," go with your gut, answer honestly, and proceed to do what is best for you with knowledge of who you are and what you wish to gain into your life. Don't make a decision more difficult than it is by overthinking. You'll thank yourself later.

FINAL THOUGHT

Question everything and resist conformity; march to the beat of your own heart, and nothing else. Make each decision as your own. Never do things out of fear or coercion. Embrace the power of the freedom to decide for yourself, and do it with confidence! Be aware of your goals, and make every decision with the mindfulness of what you strive to attract into your life.

CHAPTER 3

HOW TO B.E.E SUCCESSFUL AT ANYTHING

"The mind is the limit. As long as the mind can envision the fact that you can do something, you can do it, as long as you really believe 100 percent."

– ARNOLD SCHWARZENEGGER

B elieve you can achieve what you dare to dream. Know that you have the power to make your dreams a reality.

E nvision yourself becoming exactly who you know you can be. Close your eyes and see yourself doing exactly what you want to do.

E xecute. Make a plan and execute! No one got what they wanted by lying in bed dreaming about it. Never stop until you're the person you have the potential to be. The world is at your fingertips, just reach out and grab it.

BELIEVE

All things great and possible for yourself start and end in the mind. You will get absolutely nowhere with an idea, a thought, a hope, or dream if you do not BELIEVE it first. You may have all the support in the world and the recourses to achieve your goals, but will still fail if you don't think you can do it. If you truly believe and know in your heart that you can do something, then you can! No exceptions at all, YOU CAN. If you don't think you deserve it or think that it's even possible then you won't even begin looking for it. That's where you start. Start with the fact that you undeniably deserve what you desire most, and that's not a trick in any way. It's true, believe that it is certainly possible and you are deserving of it.

ENVISION

What do you really want? What's your goal? Now that you believe you are 110% capable of it, see yourself doing it.

Literally close your eyes and constantly envision yourself doing or being whatever it is that your dream entails. See yourself holding that trophy or diploma. In your mind, imagine making those millions of dollars, and feel the money sift through your fingertips as you count it. Feel your arms rise as you cross the finish line in first place. Really see the ocean and the feel the sand between your toes upon the beach you've always dreamt of moving to. You must play it over in your head over and over and over until the day you're physically living it.

EXECUTE

Make your plan of attack, then execute! Now that you believe you can do it and can envision yourself doing it, go out and get it! Nothing can stop you now. This last stage of your potential greatness is just as important as the others. Yeah, you can believe it and see it all you want, but if you're not doing anything about it then that's all it ever is: something you know you can do and see yourself doing, but that is trapped in the mind. Have the courage to rip it out of your mind and create the reality you see for yourself. Don't make excuses, just do it. Excuses are just made up thoughts by someone who is afraid. Don't be afraid. Be strong, courageous, and attack your dream!

Aside from why, the most important part of pursuing anything worthwhile is actually doing it. Being motivated, goal-oriented, optimistic, and purpose-driven are all fantastic mindsets, but are all absolutely worthless if you don't operationalize your ideas.

1. Don't talk. Show. Stop talking about how you're doing something, and let your results speak for themselves.

2. Don't watch. Do. Stop watching other people do things for inspiration and motivation, if you don't plan on acting on it. Take your motivational source as your coffee, and then get out there and go for it! Seeking motivation and inspiration only to continue doing nothing is like drinking a 5-hour energy right before you climb into bed. It's utterly pointless.

3. Don't just learn. Experiment. The right mindset will be the gas that fuels your intent. There's no point in filling up your car if you don't intend on ever driving it again. Be a practical researcher instead of solely observational. Notice how it says don't "just" in the opening sentence, because you should never stop thinking, dreaming, or learning. The key is to apply that knowledge to experiments out in the real world, and adapt accordingly. Remember what works for one person might not work for you.

CHALLENGE

Today (5 minutes) think of something you've had your heart set on achieving recently; a change you want to make, something you wish to possess, etc. Out loud, tell yourself that you will do it or that it will be yours. Really believe this affirmation with all of your heart. Next, close your eyes and see yourself already having or doing it. Finally, do the first thing that you know you must do to obtain it.

CHAPTER 4

VISION DECISIONS

*"If you develop the absolute sense of certainty that
powerful beliefs provide, then you can get yourself to
accomplish virtually anything, including those things
that other people are certain are impossible."*

– TONY ROBBINS

HOW TO FIX UNCERTAINTY AND INDECISIVENESS

It's effortless to fall captive to an uncertain mindset, listening to the tug of war between the voices in our head fighting over what the perfect decision is. Stay in this place too long and you'll find yourself paralyzed by the fear of making the "wrong" choice, uncertain about yourself, uncertain about your decisions, uncertain about your future. Make no mistake, there is such beauty in uncertainty; unaware of what's next is what makes life intriguingly mysterious. How often do we find ourselves being uncertain if what we're doing is right for us? How often do we doubt ourselves and find ourselves feeling indecisive and uncertain about so many external factors in our lives? The key to locking in the answer is found in the question above. It's not the uncertainty with external factors that we should concern ourselves with. It's the uncertainty of our internal factors that is the real and only problem to solve. Just like many things desired in our lives, it starts on the inside and moves outward. There is only one true certainty in life, and that is that nothing is certain. All we can do is make the best choice at hand with the information with which we are provided, and to only expect the unexpected.

Self-certainty is one of the strongest determinants of every outcome in your life. How does one feel certain? It starts with a vision, a goal, and the big picture. How certain are you of your vision? How badly to you wish to see it happen, achieve that goal, and be in that big picture? The next step is to make clear and concise decisions. How do I know if it's right or wrong? Exactly. There is no right or wrong, there is only doing. By starting small and moving grand scale is where the self-certainty will kick in like any other skill that you practice. At every moment of indecisiveness, just count to three and decide. To be crystal clear on one very important point here, without a clear vision, there can be a misguided or absence of choice altogether. If you're not deciding for yourself, then someone else is.

Everything doesn't happen at once and it doesn't have to. Trust the timing of your life and how each decision unfolds into the next. The important takeaway here is to just decide. Understand your urges, and make a decision. Success doesn't happen by accident and dreams aren't manifested out of thin air. Every decision affects the next, and everything we've done in the past has led us here, today, to this moment.

QUICK TIP

Indecisive? Text yourself your question, as if you were talking to a friend; it might sound weird, but seeing the question written down and reading it as if your friend was asking you for advice, the answer may become that much clearer to you. Usually, your first instinct is the correct one and this might be the nudge you need to get back to the path of your vision.

MAKE DECISIONS MINDFUL OF YOUR HAPPINESS

It's often the decisions that are truest to your authentic intention that are the hardest ones to make. They push us into a corner and force us to ask ourselves, "Is this what's best for me?" Once we take a step back and actually think about the answer, the answer becomes increasingly obvious. We often misinterpret the meaning of what is "best for me," because the answer is hidden within a bunch of other debris, such as what other people think is best for you, what you've been told is best for you, and what you've been forced to believe is best for you. Sift through all of the debris to find the diamond in the rough. That diamond is the answer you knew all along. It's your inner voice; it's the urge you've been itching to scratch, the temptations that you're resisting. It's you; your soul's awareness is a diamond needing to be excavated and polished to shine its true brilliance out into the world.

The fallout of making these types of decisions will hold you back from making some of them. The consequence of disappointing others is something we have to remove from the equation completely. Nobody knows what's better for you than you. The last factor is wanting what is going to make you happy. There is no decision more important than the one that will make you happy. These are the smartest decisions a human can make.

Think ahead two moves. How will this current action bring you to the one two moves from now? Are they connected, or are they just random acts? And more importantly, how will it play out in creating the vision you see? Every action without a purpose is wasted time as far as your goals are concerned, and as we know time is the most precious commodity that cannot be repeated or given back.

QUICK TIPS

1. Remember your gut instinct? What was your initial verdict? How did it make you feel?

2. Learn more about your subject. It's natural to have more questions. Do your research.

3. Write down pros and cons. A visual comparison is always a useful tool.

4. Was your gut right? Still feel the same as you did at first glance?

5. Do it! Don't overthink.

CHALLENGE

Starting today, make every decision moving forward count toward turning your dreams into a reality. Right now, make one single decision, even mentally, in the direction of your vision. Count to three, and if it feels right to you, and then do it. No thinking, just doing. One, Two, Three, Go!

CHAPTER 5

YOU ARE THE MASTER OF YOUR FATE

Whoever, other than yourself, thinks they can tell you what a good or bad choice means to you in your own life is a liar. The choice is yours alone and how it fits into your vision rests upon your shoulders. Make conscious choices and make them your own.

STOP PLAYING THE BLAME GAME

As you know, life seldom works out exactly how we planned. With this in mind, life itself isn't to blame for the absence of what we desire most. It throws in a pothole or maybe an entire sinkhole unexpectedly, but your choices dictate your life. Those who don't and have the willpower to be resourceful will contribute external factors to their failure in attempts to shift blame away from them. If you are not resourceful, you tend to blame it on lack of resources, right? The ugly truth is if you view your life as unsatisfactory, and the circumstances you're in are under your control, then the fault lies with you, not your environment.

Thomas Edison famously said, "I have not failed. I've just found 10,000 way that didn't work." It's easy to admit failure if you say, "I tried everything." Know right now that you have not. Maybe the shortcuts, easy choices, and road most traveled, but you have not tried everything if you have not yet reached your goal. With unbreakable purpose, you will find a way. If you truly with all your heart and soul desire something so passionately that it consumes your mind and body, then you will undeniably find a way. You will become resourceful. You will succeed. You'll begin to find that excuses that sound like, "I don't have enough time, I didn't have the money, I'm not good, smart, or strong enough" will all dissolve after turning attention from uncontrollable environmental factors to your own controllable choices in the face of outside influence. You will discover the time, work harder, save the money, whatever it is you need to do that is necessary to get what you want. Make no mistake, you will recognize that you ARE and WILL become resourceful enough. The choice is and always has been in your hands.

FOCUS ON YOUR BEHAVIORN INSTEAD OF YOUR GOALS

Keep this at the forefront of reminders when working toward success in anything you choose to set your mind to. Focus on what is in your control, rather than what you want the outcome to be. For example, you've moved to a new area—you want to try soccer—but you've never physically played before. Although, you know you can do it; you're fast, agile, smart, understand the rules, and how the game is played. You wish to be the captain of that team. So, one day you walk up to the coach and say "Okay, I'm captain now. I'll take it from here." I promise that three words you will never hear that coach utter next are, "Okay, sounds good."

Apply this to any circumstance. Things don't tend to happen just because you want them to. Your self-belief and confidence in your thoughts is only the beginning, important nonetheless, but only a start. Taking where you are mentally and shifting that intention toward your behaviors to mimic what is inside your head is what counts. Focus only on the next behavior that will bring you closer toward your goal instead of spending day after day questioning why you haven't accomplished it yet. Setting a goal and achieving a goal are two different things.

What you can control in your quest to become captain of that team is your performance, how much you practice, doing your job, cohesion with you teammates, your execution during game time, and most of all signing up; taking the first behavior-oriented step outside of your mind is most important. You can't be the captain if you're not even signed up for tryouts.

REMEMBER

You are the master of your fate. The proper mindset coupled with mirrored actions will see yourself becoming and achieving whatever you can dream. Stop making excuses and control what comes next. Only you can decide.

CHAPTER 6

CONVERTING FEAR TO FIRE

ACHIEVEMEPHOBIA: FEAR OF SUCCESS

Strange concept? Who doesn't want to be successful, right? Not as strange as you may think. The genesis of this psychological crisis can be attributed to a fear of change and the possibility of being unable to handle what comes with it. You may be so comfortable living within the parameters of the life you've built that changing it begins to scare you a little. If success were a backpack, inside it are responsibilities, fear of failure, potentially letting others down, not living up to expectations, limelight, endless new personal developments and breaking out of your shell. You can see how the straps begin to weigh heavier, cutting into your shoulders.

No worries. It's curable and it's all part of the process. When are we really 100% ready to do anything? If we waited until the timing was perfect for anything, we wouldn't get anywhere, or get anything done. It's all about putting one foot forward and letting the other one follow. Adaptation and evolution are the cornerstones of any journey, and you will find that stepping out of your comfort zone is located right at the top of your to-do list.

This psychological crisis can also be linked to the Imposter Syndrome, a term meaning that people who absolutely deserve everything and more are afraid to express their voice or idea to the world, because they think they are unworthy of the success. These people often think that they aren't as smart or deserving as others see them to be, even though they are clearly high-achieving individuals for even sparking the idea of innovation in their own original work.

GO ALL-IN

If you have an idea or a thought that's swimming in your head, but are hesitant to act because of self-doubt, just do it and worry about what comes next when you cross that bridge. The only thing worse than failing is stalling. If you stall, you waste time, and that is our most valuable form or currency and commodity. If you have the potential within you or you see the potential within something else, you have to jump right in.

Hesitation is the death of dreams. Fail to act and see yourself at your dream's funeral looking upon what could have been, laying lifeless in the casket. Throw yourself passionately and completely into whatever it is you do. If that means taking more classes, reading more books, webinars, meetings, networking, spending money to obtain more knowledge and advancement of your progress, it is time and money well spent. While you're doing all of this experimenting and learning, you're already light-years ahead of the person that's still sitting on his couch, saying to himself "I think I'd be good at that," or "maybe I'll try that out, but not right now."

DEFLATING YOUR DOUBTS

Anyone with dreams of something magnificent by the sole desire to make it a reality deserves to be created. It's no secret that we can ask ourselves questions such as, "What makes me good, strong, powerful, etc. enough to do this?" Every dreamer has doubts. What your doubts are fighting to overpower the sound of is the truth. The truth is that you ARE worth it. There IS someone out there who cares. You ARE capable. Any success aspirer is deserving of the dream they dare to manifest.

Think about this. If even one person expresses interest, enthusiasm, or the slightest intrigue into what you have to offer, then thinking that reading your "stupid" book, listen to your "dumb" idea, or buying your "worthless" product; it might not be that stupid, dumb, or worthless after all. The fact that you can impact one person's life by your actions while bettering your own should be enough for you to get over any terrors you may harbor inside.

QUICK TIP

Whenever you feel self-sabotaging thoughts attempting to wedge their way between your capable mind and your dream, stop them immediately and ask yourself **"Why not me?"** After finding no such answer to that question (because there is none. You deserve and will have everything you desire if you make it so), say to yourself **"that will be me,"** and continue with your plan.

CHALLENGE

This week, do something that you've been scared to do because of limiting beliefs. Anything at all that frightens you to step out of that comfort zone, DO IT...don't think, just do. Mark it down in your calendar, set an alarm, whatever you have to do that ensures your follow-through, just do it.

CHAPTER 7

UNCOVERING YOUR PASSION

"The two most important days of your life are the day you were born and the day you find out why"

– MARK TWAIN

I implore you to entertain the idea that your passion isn't lost in needing of finding. It's been with you all along. It just needs a coercing to bring itself to light. Do not play hide and seek with passion anymore like others may suggest. Rather, turn your attention inward because it has already found you. All you need to do is listen and uncover it. It is always there and it has always been there; a gentle whisper, a flickering ember waiting to be ignited and for the life of you mustn't be ignored. It is the core purpose of our soul to embrace the fire the drives our desires and allows us to let it lead us on the adventure it has in store.

MAKE MUSIC, NOT NOISE

Let your days be guided by music contrary to noise. Huh? Well, your passion, what you do, your "thing" is the instrument and what you do with it creates the music. You just have to find the right instrument. Doing what you love, and turning it into what you DO creates flow. Flow, as said by Mihaly Csikszentmihalyi is, "The mental state of operation in which a person performing an activity is fully immersed in a feeling of energized focus, full involvement, and enjoyment in the process of the activity."

Flow allows you to be lost in a task that burns your soul, that the concept of time is irrelevant, and before you know it, five hours have passed, but it felt like ten minutes. Every one of us has experienced this while doing tasks we excel in and that we enjoy. Flow is the sweet spot where your skill level meets the challenge of the task, allowing you to be adrift in the current of productivity.

Noise, on the other hand, is everything we do that deters us from our passion. Everything that takes time from you dedicating yourself to what you love are nails on a chalkboard. Leading a life in which you are doing things because of external pressures or settling will create the feeling of listening to that song you hate on the radio over and over, and over, and over, and over. It's up to you to simply change the station. The goal is to wake up every day doing what you love, isn't it? "Yeah, but it's not that simple" is a common response to that question. Breaking news. Yes, it is indeed that simple, but there's also a catch. It takes time and experimentation. You can't just reach into a hat and find a passion to follow. It takes molding, nurturing, trying, failing, liking, disliking, and exploring to sift through other distractions in order to uncover what's beneath the surface. Create your masterpiece; let each day play as music to your ears. Uncover your passion.

KNOW WHAT YOU ARE GOOD AT

Do we agree that we all love doing things we're good at? It feels good to do something well. It's enjoyable and boosts productivity. So why not find a way to incorporate it into your everyday life. If you are driven deeply by something you hold close to your heart, you need to explore that, and figure out how you can plug that into your life moving forward. Satisfying hobbies shouldn't always be reserved for special times and occasions. Any day that you are alive is a special occasion. Don't waste it! Hone in on what stirs your curiosity rooted in your strengths, and focus on improving in those areas rather than giving more energy to what you're bad at.

"Whether you're 9 or 90, stop trying to fix the things you're bad at and focus on the things you're good at ."

– GARY VAYNERCHUK

Establishing strengths and weaknesses is a phenomenal start. What comes next is realizing that it takes hard work and dedication just like anything beautiful, brilliant, and worthwhile in your life. Whatever is worth having never comes easily. The key is to make your passion work for you. Let it be the motivation you need to get out of bed, make it be the thing you look forward to the most tomorrow, and let it drive you. If you love something enough you will find a way to make it work.

"Look for a situation in which your work will give you as much happiness as your spare time"

– PABLO PICASSO

KNOW WHAT YOU ARE BAD AT

This task is far more difficult than listing things you're good at, mainly because it requires a brutally honest self-audit. It's a comforting thought to shower ourselves with thoughts about all of the things at which we excel, and what is satisfying to us. Finding out what you absolutely do not wish to pursue is just as important as realizing what you do want to go forward with. It may be that you think you will get better when you know you just do not have the skills. You may think you're stuck and have no choice but to make a negative into a positive. It's hard to admit we're bad at anything; it's uncomfortable, embarrassing, and it makes us feel weak. Especially, when we are in the midst of actually doing it. The problem often doesn't lay with our will power, or willingness to try. It's due to lack of awareness of your natural talents and forcing yourself into something that causes you to doubt your place in the world.

Guiding yourself to your passions is like buying a car on a lot. You're looking for a sports car, but unsure of make, model, color, etc. Salesman asks, "You said that you definitely want a sports car, but not sure of the make or model yet?" You reply with an enthusiastic, yes. He then says, "Great, I have it narrowed down, follow me. It's either the Mustang or the Minivan." Wait, what? Doesn't really leave you with much of a choice, other than knowing 100%, for sure, absolutely for a fact that the Minivan is out of the question (no offense to Minivan owners). Steer yourself into the right direction by steering away from the wrong one first.

Identifying weaknesses can be just as easy as identifying strengths, but your ego may take a few punches in the process. The key here is to understand that you are not stupid or incapable of achieving your dreams. Never allow negativity to diminish your confidence and lead you to believe you're anything less than amazing in your own right. At what, is for you to figure out.

> *" Everybody is a Genius. But If You Judge a Fish by Its Ability to Climb a Tree, It Will Live Its Whole Life Believing that It is Stupid. "*
>
> – ALBERT EINSTEIN

FIND YOUR NICHE

Write down a list of things that you're good at, that you enjoy doing: your hobbies, actions that bring you happiness. Then, write down things you're bad at, things that you dread doing, actions that create stress and general responses of unhappiness. Continue on to highlighting something you're great at and find much joy in. Nobody said you had to be good at everything to succeed massively. All it takes is being especially great at one thing. Highlight your strengths, experiment, and find your specialty.

Skill specialization will beat out generalization any day of the week. Make your skills deeper, not wider. Find your niche and work on it. If your air conditioning is broken and you have two business cards reading, "John: I fix things" and "John's Air Conditioning Repair." Which one do you choose for your specific demand? There is always a demand, so become the supply.

BE GREAT

Don't be the person who wants to be **just** something. Be the person who wants to be a **great** something. Don't just set out to do something, set out to do something great. You don't run a race hoping to come in forth, so why shouldn't everything else in your life be done any differently? Whatever you do, enter with the mindset of being great.

This is where knowing your strengths, finding out what you love, and finding a niche come into play. If you love math and your dream is to tutor people who aren't good at it, then all you have to do is be better than the people you are trying to teach. You're not going to go out and tutor college mathematics if you failed every course while you were an undergrad. If that's truly what makes you happy, then focus on tutoring for elementary or high school math instead. There is something in the world there for everyone, you just have to find where you fit in.

EMBRACE YOUR UNIQUENESS

You need to be at peace with yourself and who you are. Embrace all that is you, inside and out. It is not an accident that you are here and have been given the gifts that you have. None of us are alike, and will all follow a different path to get to where we are going. Similar to finding out what you love, and what you want to do with it moving forward. The most important key to achieving self-discovery is not giving a shit about your weaknesses because nobody else does. The only person that can dwell on your weaknesses enough to hold them back is you. Feeling self-conscious about our weaknesses is unacceptable, unbecoming, and will ultimately stump your personal development until you learn to re-shape your mindset.

The hardest judge of your actions is you. That's the problem with seeking success in any area of our lives; once you start improving, you will never be satisfied until you deem it perfect. Strive for greatness in everything you do, but never to be perfect. Progress is more important than perfection. Place one foot in front of the other and do not stop until you have reached your goals.

QUICK TIP

Make a list of your strengths and weaknesses when approaching new endeavors. This may help clarify where you need to spend the most time in your progression. What do you lose yourself and sense time doing? Don't ignore it. Explore it.

CHAPTER 8

ARE YOU WALKING THE WALK OR JUST TALKING THE TALK?

COMMIT

This word is everything. Commit yourself not only to your dream, but also a commitment to others, success, goals, etc. All of these will soon follow suit as soon as you commit to the person that matters the most in the grand scheme of all of it: YOU. First and foremost, commit to yourself, or none of the above can be made possible! There's only one simple rule to follow to obtain whatever is in your sights. Brace yourself, here it is...

Tell yourself you're going to do something, then DO IT!

How do you expect to commit to anything else before committing to and carrying out your own promises? Anybody can talk a lot of shit, but it takes a genuinely purpose-driven person in the pursuit of their dreams to actually back it up.

There are countless ways to deceive others with excuses, and "coulda, shoulda, woulda's." These are veils created to disguise the fact that we never really committed to the task in the first place, and are simply just talking the talk. We often say things like "I was going to do (insert intention here), but..." and then never end up doing it because of some excuse you make in the absence of our actions and true commitment to your cause.

It is impossible to deceive yourself! Only you know what lies behind the veil and can commit to what you set in front of you. All can dream, but only the brave can carry out the conviction necessary to materialize it into a reality. Deeply and fully commit to the task and see your efforts take flight or fall to their demise, but you must commit yourself. This one simple word can make or break you. So... what's it going to be?

QUICK TIP

Hold yourself accountable for the promises you make by marking off a specific date or time that you will complete a task towards your goal.

CHAPTER 9

DON'T BE AFRAID TO FLY

"Everyone forgets that Icarus also flew...
I believe Icarus was not failing as he fell, but just
coming to the end of his triumph"

– JACK GILBERT

Don't be afraid to fly. Failure is only found in the absence of attempt. The mere fact that you have the fortitude to try is a triumph on its own, and should be viewed as nothing less. To paraphrase Jack Gilbert's excerpt above: Correct, Icarus fell, but he also flew. Everyone forgets that part. Even if you fail at first, you win every single time against the people who fail to try. Perspective is everything. Choose how you see the world, change your thoughts and change your life.

Our paths to triumph in any area of our lives must be paved with risks. Who the hell is anyone to tell you that you have failed, if you had the courage to try? Wholeheartedly take that leap off of the cliff of fear and into the sea of uncertainty. The only time we truly fail is when we do not try. By failing to jump, you have already deprived yourself of the adventure of the fall, and what you learn about yourself on the way down. That's the beauty of life, for we don't have to get it right, we just have to try.

Risk and fear are closely associated. Fear is the number one factor of not taking risks; the fear of not being good enough, fear of failure, fear of judgment, fear of change. Taking that leap means doing exactly that, just close your eyes and jump. You don't need a planned intervention to conquer those fears, because they're self-created. You wouldn't even have a thought about achieving something great if something inside you didn't believe it. Whatever voice inside you led you to think about doing something great for yourself, find that voice and hold onto it as your guide.

"Fear is not real. It is a product of thoughts you create.
Do not misunderstand me. Danger is
very real. But fear is a choice."

– WILL SMITH

It all starts by heaving yourself into the unknown with the passion you burn with for the goal you aim to accomplish. Risk comes with potential loss, but hope to yield gain. Hope is the key word in any meaningful endeavor. None of us would take any risks if we weren't hopeful of a positive outcome. If you are unaware of what is at risk for you, then you are blind, not afraid. Awareness of what you stand to lose and what you may gain will tell you all you need to know about the risk you are contemplating.

CHALLENGE!

If you can think it, you can do it; Cliché, but true all the same. Close your eyes, and think of something you really want, but are hesitant to go after for whatever excuse you're making. Now open your eyes, and draw what was in your mind into a thought bubble attached to a little stick figure that represents you, whether it's a picture or words, get it in there. Then draw outwardly in separate circles all the different ways that lead you to get to whatever you wrote in that bubble. Then, ask yourself what's the biggest and boldest move you can make right now to get you from where you are to what you wrote in that thought bubble. Do that tomorrow! Do it without a second thought.

CHAPTER 10

MAKE IT HAPPEN

The time has come for you stop stewing in thoughts of what's to come and what you wish to see in front of you. The time has come to act. Take your thoughts from the abstract land of the mind and project them into your life. Now is the time to devise your master plan, coupling it with massive action. You've made it to the starting line, now explode off of it and dominate.

GETTING IT OUT OF YOUR HEAD

Rubbing a lamp doesn't manifest a genie granting your wishes. That's only in Aladdin. It's brought into reality though by taking hold of and tearing the abstract idea from your mind and putting it down on paper for you to see. That's the first step. Actually seeing your goals laid out for your eyes to see makes it that much more real. Some people do not even get that far. Passive Dreamers only dream. They imagine a perfect movie in which they are the main character. Visualization is a crucial technique, but it doesn't make your dream any more real than a dream until you do something about becoming that character. Become an Active Dreamer. Get your dreams out of your head and in front of you. Start here and begin to see your vision follow quickly upon heel.

EXPERIMENT

Any great objective requires a foolproof plan to achieve it. The key is to find a proven path that has worked before. Create an experiment, gather your hypothesis, divulge a plan of action based on something that has been proven to work before, and then get to work. Nobody said you get it right on the first try. That's what experimentation is about. The more you try, the less you need to hypothesize. It's similar with multiple-choice questions, you have to weed out what absolutely doesn't work for your question until you stumble upon the correct answer. People often treat goals like a dart-throwing balloon game. For those who have never played, it goes like this: There is a wooden wall covered with inflated balloons, and behind one of the balloons is a sticker that says you've won a prize, you take darts to throw at these balloons in hope that you will hit the one with the prize sticker behind it. A well-constructed plan to make your goal a reality is the only way such a thought is possible without wasting valuable time and resources. Not throwing darts at balloons.

MAKE UNSTOPPABLE PLANS

You have your goal in mind and the burning passion to achieve it. You've tried and saw what worked and what didn't work so far. You can now feel yourself gaining speed. Now that you're over the hump of knowing what you want, seeing it before you, and an idea of how to get it, it's time to run downhill.

Have exact objectives, not ambiguous hopes. For example, instead of "I hope something works out by Friday," say, and write down exactly what you're going to do leading up to Friday, and let Friday be the day you cross it off your list, not the day where your questions yield an unknown answer hoping for the best. By having exact goals in mind, it's easier to play out a blueprint for achieving them.

1. Number the steps.
Under the numbering, write, "if not, then (insert backup plan)." For example:

1.) Do this.
1a.) **If not, then** try this...

State what you will do as a contingency plan. Do this until something works. If plan A doesn't go accordingly, there's 25 more letters in the alphabet.

2. Create a Goal Calendar. If there is one important cliff note to take from this chapter, this is it. Whether the calendar is on your phone, on your wall, drawing one; it doesn't matter how but just have one in front of you!

Step 1: Establish your Success Date.

Step 2: This is important. Think long and hard about approximately how long your journey will be in making your dream a reality; if that sounded dramatic, good, because it is. I can't stress how important this is. As we talked about before, time is one of the things you can never have back, so plan accordingly and make it count.

Step 3: Once you've circled, highlighted, starred, hearted your success date, find the date you are currently on today and write what you are going to do. Start immediately, time doesn't wait for us to get our shit together. Start whether you're ready or not, just start (it's often the hardest part).

Step 4: At your choosing, start filling in your calendar with objectives for each day or week depending on the time you're willing to spend at a given time. At the end of each week you should write in a different color to make it visibly important that you've completed your weekly objective. Like anything worthwhile, it is a process, it will be long, but pride cannot be replaced by any other feeling in the world.

3. Make S.M.A.R.T. Goals.
Specific: Define your goal as elaborately as possible without using ambiguity.

Measurable: Does your plan keep track of your outcomes as you advance?

Attainable: Is your goal reasonable enough to be accomplished? Make sure your goal is reasonable; baby steps, baby steps, baby steps.
Relevant: Is it worthwhile? Does it relate to your overall vision?
Timely: Do you have a clear and concise date that you will complete it? Do you have a sense of urgency about your goal?

COUNTERPUNCHING

"Everyone has a plan until they get punched in the face"

– MIKE TYSON

True. The key here is to learn how to counterpunch. Make no mistake; there will be a lightning fast punch that catches you unaware, making you see stars. Punches such as these will have you questioning why the hell you even stepped into the ring in the first place. This is one of those punches that you will never see coming no matter how good of a plan you had. The famous phrase is that you have to "roll with the punches." When life decides to hit you with a quick combination, you have to take that punch for what it is: a superior punch that has slipped through your guard, and now it's time to seamlessly regroup and fire one back.

Your plans will continuously require you to regroup, rethink, and retest, and even restart if necessary. Once you've had an idea that you truly believe in, and you've reached the point of no return, it's your duty to see it through to success or defeat. What's even worse than not following through with your plan is holding on to a lost cause. Sometimes having the awareness to recognize that something just isn't going to work after the trial and error of every possible angle is hard because you want it to work so badly. Since emotional investment can obstruct an objective view, holding on, in some cases can hurt you more than letting go. It's important to know the difference and when to do so.

CHALLENGE

Sit down today and create your Goal Calendar! Whether they are goals for the week, goals for the month, or goals for the year. Every night, starting tonight write down what you intend to accomplish the next day.

CHAPTER 11

SHORT-AND LONG-TERM GOALS

SHORT-TERM

Short-term goals are equally as important as your end state goal. These are the goals that snowball right into your dream. In chess, you have to have a mindset for the future, and be mindful of your opponents, with individual moves leading to the one that ideally concludes the match in checkmate.

1. Little Victories

Nobody wants to continue anything for too long if all they know is failure at every attempt. The calendar keeping track of your progress is a fail-safe way to keep you on track, providing you with exciting new challenges each week.

Small victories will build joy in attacking your day, leading to excitement levels that you've only ever felt while doing something you absolutely love doing. By never reaching short-term goals in the pursuit of something larger and more meaningful can result in the exact opposite of what you're searching for. This is why the A in setting SMART goals is so important. Attainable goals will give you the short-term satisfaction of winning each time you hit a checkpoint on the path to something great.

2. Fall in Love

Fall in love with the journey, not just the destination. They say if you love what you do you'll never work a day in your life. Put your heart into each week and remain optimistic, and failure is impossible. In seminars, classes and lectures, there's always a take home point. This is the same with your journey to success. If you love the process, you will take something away that will sharpen your wisdom for your next endeavor then time was not lost or wasted, but time used perfectly.

LONG-TERM

1. Meaningful Pursuits vs. Fleeting Pleasures.

Meaningful pursuits are far more satisfying for authentic, intrinsic happiness vs. fleeting pleasures that we falsely stamp happiness onto. For example, saying "When I graduate I'll be happy, when I get that job I'll be happy, when I get healthy I'll be happy," won't create happiness, but instead fleeting pleasure that will only lead us to our next empty assumption. You soon will return to your baseline of happiness regardless of positive or negative life events. The act of longing for it creates the assumption that you will become happy once you possess it. Achieving what you believe will make you happy forces you to search for bigger and better happiness once you come down from the high of your previous pursuit.

2. Remembering Your WHY

Of course there's nothing wrong with wanting bigger and better things for yourself. It's healthy to set, achieve goals, and keep moving forward in attempts to chase every dream you've ever had. The problem arises when you depend on that goal for achieving authentic happiness. You must find happiness within the journey of getting there. Finding a strong definitive purpose will provide meaning to your goal and the reason the big picture of achieving it matters to you. A feeling such as this does not fade fast. This is what you want to stick with you: a lasting, impactful goal that will add positive value to your life, inside and out.

QUICK TIP

Lay to rest each night with a goal in mind for the following day. Awaken enthusiastically with a plan driven to make it happen. You don't have to move mountains. Just something to be able to look back on the day knowing you're 24 hours closer to achieving something great.

CHAPTER 12

AT WHAT COST?

The amazing fact of the matter is that it is indeed possible to possess all that your imagination can fathom. Now, the question that beckons is, at what cost? The good news is that this isn't the Old Testament of the Bible. You won't be asked to sacrifice your first son, but you will have to be prepared to take a rain check for other things in your life that can be identified as a luxury item. Greatness isn't free. Are you ready to make the sacrifices necessary to reach desired heights?

TIME

The amount of time that you will have to devote to achieving your greatest aspirations might be staggering, depending on the value it holds in your life. This is where your WHY comes into play again. Prioritizing your life means whatever fills the number one spot on your list is most likely also where you will be spending the bulk of your productivity efforts and hours.

Contemplating it all day and night while you're off doing other things makes you simply a dreamer, not a doer. You need to possess the facilities to become both. Binging on Netflix may have to be cut down to "maybe I can fit in an episode next week if I have the time." The new season of (insert show) can and will have to wait. You can use things like this as reward for hitting checkpoints in your goal calendar. As most of us do, we work, go to school, have children, etc. I'm not saying give your kids away, quit your job, or drop out of school (unless you want to, no judgment). The point is that you will need to cut out little blocks of time each day to work on your goals. This means cutting out some leisure/luxury time to work on your possessing what you desire most of all. If your leisure time is what you desire most, then do what you need to do to possess more of that instead.

Life isn't simple. Life is messy and unorganized, and with what control you do have, time management is an important cornerstone. With that said, no two humans are alike. For instance, some may be able to quit their jobs and devote all of their time to their dreams, while others may have to work three jobs to make ends meet. Some do not have children, which is the most important job of all since it is no longer your life that comes first. It's theirs. Some of us do not attend school. The bottom line is that you must tailor your program and time according to your own life and what's in it. There is no blanket guide to success, and how to achieve it; only suggestions, guidelines, and tools given to you to build the life you crave with the time you make to do it.

MONEY

Bringing a dream into reality requires you to obtain and use different resources in order to achieve it. Realistically, what's the number one thing that we all need in order to do anything tangible in exchange for what we want? MONEY.

So, we took away your Netflix, and now it's time to take away some money. Why are you still reading if you know you have to give up time and money? Did you close the book? No? Great, then you've just answered the questions above and more. This means your DREAM is more important than your luxuries and frivolous spending. Your reason for achieving what you want is more important than (some) time and (some) money. With that said, reaching your goals may require you to spend money on whatever resources you need, according to each of your personalized goals. If getting fit and living healthier is your vision, we can then assume your money will go towards healthy foods, gym membership, personal training, etc. One of the few things in life we CAN get back is money, whether it's in the form of actual currency, or in the intrinsic sense by the return on your investment into the vision of your dream life.

RELATIONSHIPS

This one is to be treaded lightly. By no degree am I suggesting becoming reclusive and throwing away priceless human connections. We exist to coexist. It's absolutely necessary for our physiological and psychological wellbeing. The point is that you may be required to make certain sacrifices at times if your dream means enough to you. If that means accepting your dream job across the country, or hanging out with friends one fewer time per week than you usually do, then so be it. Time, money, and relationships are all interrelated. Relationships require TIME spent, money requires TIME spent (working), and TIME is something we have so little of in this one shot we get at life. It's the greatest paradox of them all, isn't it? Next year feels like forever away, but last year feels like yesterday.

If the relationship is as important as you understand it to be, then it will last through however much it is meant to. Tough don't last, but tough people do. Understand that the people you love do love you back and want to see you succeed as much as they themselves do. This is ultimately the hardest sacrifice for success that we all face one day. Following your dreams sometimes means physically following them to wherever they take you. If you truly want your dream to become a reality, make sure you do everything in your power to fight to make it happen. Losing is not an option and neither is losing touch with those close to us.

 REMINDER
Do not misinterpret the word sacrifice for abandonment. Yes, dreams require sacrifice, but they also require balance. Your health, your relationships, your social life, and your happiness are just as important. There's no fun in success if you're not happy and there's no one around to share it with.

CHAPTER 13

SURROUND YOURSELF WITH EXCELLENCE

Summary in a sentence: What you surround yourself with is what you become; it will raise you up or drag you down.

You do not become an Olympic swimmer by training for a foot race, hanging out with sprinters, studying great runners, and then asking yourself why you still suck at swimming. The same metaphor can be applied to your own life and what you to wish attract into it by what you choose to be surrounded by. As discussed before, a mindset, talent, and dreams can only carry you so far. It's an outstanding start, but that's not all the pieces to the puzzle. You have to commit to it in every aspect of your life. Ask yourself the simple question, "Am I honestly putting myself in the best position for success and happiness in my life?"

Now it's time to evaluate your surroundings and who is included.

Making sure that what you're surrounding yourself with matches your vision, and recognize that it is of the utmost importance to your outcome. From the people you have in your life, the area in which you live, and the activities you do, to the hobbies that consume your time; it all matters, and it must add positive value in support of your personal mission. To truly change your life in the pursuit of success and sustainability, it's not like a job that you drive to and once you're done for the day, you go home. Nope, not that simple I'm afraid.

CREATING YOUR PICTURE PERFECT PUZZLE

Anyone and everyone can piece together the life they've always wanted one puzzle piece at a time. What's the easiest part of a puzzle to put together: The border, what surrounds that core picture you're trying to create.

Our lives are theoretically translated in the same way; in the sense that who we are and what we want is surrounded by the environment that we create for ourselves. Place yourself in the middle of what you wish to be surrounded by for your success. Committing to your dream full-time greatly involves and is impacted by your surroundings. Your dreams work from the inside out and then reflect from the outside in. Everything must be like looking in a mirror. The reflection must resemble what you wish to attract into your life.

THE WRONG PEOPLE

Watch your back while ascending the staircase of success; you never know who's concealing a knife. Believe it or not, not everyone wants to see you succeed. The world does not revolve around you and you know that, but sadly there are people out there who think they're the sun and in turn, earth orbits them. By you succeeding, achieving a sense of purpose, happiness, and fulfillment in life means that you have stolen a bit of "their" success, and this stirs jealousy. Jealousy is an ugly emotion that brings out the worst in a person.

The point here isn't to be paranoid, but aware. Be mindful who is by your side when you're down, and who's there when you make your ascent. Notice those who praise and encourage your success, and are genuinely happy for your growth. Be aware of those others who condemn it, hold contempt in the light of your rise, and attempt to block you from it. Let their hate fuel your fire. Make it in spite of them, but give no energy to it. Avoid negative people at all costs. They will only drag you down. Misery loves company.

THE RIGHT PEOPLE

Surrounding yourself with people is easy; there are over 7 billion of them out there. The important part finding the right ones for you.

"Surround yourself with people who make you happy. People who make you laugh, who help you when you're in need, People who genuinely care. They are the ones worth keeping in your life. Everyone else is just passing through. "

– KARL MARX

Surrounding yourself with genuine, authentic, and like-minded individuals is more important than you may realize. Simply being in the presence of those who have the desire to achieve something great and the drive to do so will inspire your own. If you're around lazy people; you become lazy. If you surround yourself with fit and healthy people, you will adapt and evolve to become fit and healthy. This works with every example you want to plug it into going in both directions. <u>The people around you will either raise or lower your standards. Period.</u>

QUICK TIPS

1. Have all levels of expertise located within your peer groups

What's important is to surround yourself not only with peers with similar aspirations but to include others who are far ahead of you and where you hope to be one day, and lastly, with those beneath your level of experience to give you a chance to lead someone who one day hopes to standing in your shoes. Giving direction to others with the knowledge they hope to obtain is a valuable habit in personal growth.

Others learn not always from your teaching, but from by seeing you learn. Taking notice to a successful person's process is just as important as taking their direction.

Learn, teach, and lead by example. Gelling interactions with multi-leveled groups will provide valuable knowledge on path to positive progression.

2. Do not lose yourself in someone else's reflection

"Be yourself. Everyone else is already taken!"

– OSCAR WILDE

Anyone who has achieved anything truly great like your favorite inventor, thinker, athlete, entrepreneur, or role model has been like a sponge to someone(s) he or she aspires to learn from. Aspiring to be like someone else does not mean **becoming** someone else. We are all graced with our own talents, personality, and skill-set for a reason. We're meant to be what we're meant to be, not to be a clone of someone else. We are not copies of those who we wish to study, rather a unique and special individual capable of anything with the right sense of self and awareness of who we are and where we want to go. Admiring qualities and ethics of successful individuals is a great starting point to creating something unique in your own life.

3. Be your BEST self
The hard part isn't finding the types of people who set you up to bring the best out of you, but being one of these people. By being the very person you wish to have in your life, this will naturally attract the same. The Law of Attraction is powerful. Honesty with yourself and

your goals will land you in the middle of whatever you desire to attract into your life. Be the real you, the authentic you. Don't change yourself to somebody's liking. Never let others' opinions influence the weight of your own. Be who you are and you will attract people who will care for you, support you, and authentically love you for you. Be the right person for someone else's journey as well as your own. Don't be afraid to stop and ask yourself what value you're bringing to those around you in your life. An introspective reflection is always necessary.

4. Similar aspirations do not mean similar personalities.

Group members will always rub off on one another. Your surroundings as well as who's in them should challenge you and bring out the best in you, and you in them. Remember, by someone being in your life means that you are also in theirs. A community is only as good as the sum of its parts. Everyone should influence and add value to each other's lives in a positive way.

Maybe Jill has overflowing confidence, but you don't. Just being around her confidence will in time help you with yours. Maybe you have an unrelenting competitiveness that Jack lacks. Jack will in turn learn to adapt and bring up his weaknesses. Life is all about adaption and evolution. How well you adapt and change to your surroundings can slingshot you in the right direction, or have you running in quicksand.

CHALLENGE

1. Express to someone you look up to that you admire a certain quality that they possess, and then ask him or her to describe in a quick sentence of how you can come to grow in that area. Next, do something that day that relates to what that person suggested.

2. Find someone at a lesser skill level than you aspiring in the same area, then, in a sentence, teach them how to take the next step and get to the next level. Challenge them to do something related to what you have just suggested.

CHAPTER 14

BECOME A MAGNET: THINK IT. SPEAK IT. FEEL IT.

"You have absolute control over but one thing, and that's your thoughts."

– NAPOLEON HILL

Success is something you attract more than something you seek. If happiness is the goal, then <u>success is just collateral attraction.</u>

1. THINK IT

MINDSET IS EVERYTHING. The power of your thoughts can spark or extinguish a problem before you even take action. It's as simple as math. By placing a " + " or " - " in front of a number, it automatically gives you the next plan of action in solving the problem, and a hint at the outcome all in a single glance. Your mind is no different.

The Problem: your thoughts.
The Solution: your thoughts.

You need to get out of your own way when it comes to attracting desires into your life. Your thoughts about where you want to go, who you wish to be, and how to get exactly what you desire must be aligned with what you visualize for yourself when your close your eyes.

Having a positive mindset even before things get rough, knowing that they will along the way and accepting it is makes all the difference when it's forth an inches and the rough stuff hits you head-on. Realistically, we don't live in a dreamland where adversity doesn't exist. It's not a matter of if it will happen to you, only a matter of when. How you confront it will determine fight or flight. Your parasympathetic nervous system will always want to "fight" that adversity if you mind is prepared for it. Your mind is unbelievably strong and will never back down in a fight for your success if you are prepared for it with a strong enough purpose behind it. Your mental attitude can take you that extra step that separates you from turning and running or powering through.

"What we are today comes from our thoughts of yesterday, and our present thoughts build our life of tomorrow: Our life is the creation of our mind."

– BUDDHA

Anything and everything in our lives yesterday, today, and tomorrow is a manifestation of our thoughts. What you give your energy to; you will become, and is what you shall be surrounded by.

QUICK TIP

Approach every endeavor like this: Decide what you want, hope for the best, prepare for the worst, expect nothing, and be grateful for everything. A positive mindset never hurt anybody, but a negative one could destroy everything, leaving only ruins.

2. SPEAK IT

Speak into existence whatever you wish to attract into your life. By saying it aloud you are already one step closer to obtaining it. Start by hearing yourself saying exactly what you want, and make every decision moving forward mindful of your vision. Work tenaciously though your goals, and stay positive though the process.

Do this and success is inevitable. Speak of something as if you already have it. Speak about it like if you don't have it, and then you soon will. Speak about WHEN you will do/have/complete what you desire, not IF you will. Such a powerfully positive tool cannot go unused in your journey.

QUICK TIP

Approach every endeavor like this: Practice saying out loud, daily, exactly what you want for yourself. Write them down and say them out loud. Positive reassurance can mean all the difference when external stressors may begin to cloud your confidence.

The power of a single word can change the whole trajectory of your mindset. Here it is: YET. Take careful notice to how you speak about yourself and your goals to other people. You may not realize that you are creating moats around your goals without ever realizing it, and how quickly you can build a bridge to them by fixing it with one word. Reprogram yourself to say "YET" after every self-sabotaging negative thought that your mind might wander toward.

TRY THIS!

If you notice yourself saying phrases like:

"I don't get this."

"I can't do this."

"This isn't working."

"I haven't done that."

"I'm not good enough."

Start each of those sentences over, add "yet" to the end of them, and watch how things begin to change.

"I don't get this...yet."
"I can't do this...yet."
"This isn't working...yet."
"I haven't done that...yet."

3. FEEL IT

After deciding what it is that you want and speaking it into your world, now you need to feel it deep in your bones. Feel yourself already in possession of what you are aiming to attract. Feel the satisfaction that you will have when you accomplish what you set your mind to. Feel the pride that your actions will bring. Feel your goals and plans coming together in your gut and become excited at the rewards to come! With each breath, inhale and exhale with the feeling of your desires in hand. Close your eyes and really feel this because it's coming your way. It's only a matter of time!

CHALLENGE

1. Imagine/write a short story about yourself in the near future already having all of what you desire. What does it feel like? Describe that. Where are you? Describe it. What are you doing every day? Describe that.

2. Speak to at least one person and tell them what you WILL be accomplishing soon. If they ask how, tell them exactly how and really feel it in your heart that you are speaking the truth. One day it will be. Do this once a day. Choose your goal and become a magnet.

CHAPTER 15

THE POWERFUL P'S OF PRODUCTIVITY

It is imperative to possess these following P's in the pursuit of a successful and productive life. The road to fulfilling a dream is undoubtedly stricken with potholes and speed bumps. Obstacles are to be expected, but what you do next once you encounter them is what matters most. Persevere, be persistent, and maintain positivity. This is what will set you apart from the pack. Keep pushing forward. Be confident in your thoughts, follow through with action, and I promise that there will not be an outcome that you cannot create.

"Ambition is the path to success.
Persistence is the vehicle you arrive in."

– BILL BRADLEY

It's about getting out there and creating outcomes, not wishing for them. If you are truly passionate about your vision and possess the motivation for continuous follow through despite the challenges that lay ahead, then you will achieve the success you desire every single step along the way, guaranteed.

Yes, you will get rejected. Yes, you hit walls in our progress. Yes, negativity and self-doubt will be right on your heels with every step.

The key is that we mustn't let any of it deter us from the destination we want to reach. Rejection? Try again. Speed bump? Drive over it. Negativity? Replace it with positivity and seeing silver linings.

1. POSITIVITY

You have to face adversity, negativity, and disheartening circumstances to be able to combat them with the positivity that will carry the torch of your dreams and make them the reality you see in your mind. There is no success without struggle. An optimistic mindset will make the impossible seem possible, and that's all you need is to plant the seed of self-belief and to set you in the right direction. Such a powerful word has the ability to combat the darkest hours. Trust that you will make it and you will.

"Life is 10% what happens to you and 90% of how you react to it."

– CHARLES R. SWINDOLL

---

2 AND 3. PERSEVERANCE AND PERSISTENCE

The image that really resonates with me is of the one where there are two men in separate frames digging for diamonds. We can see that the diamonds are just inches away, if only they would both dig for a few more minutes. The man in the left frame gives up and turns to leave. The man in the right frame continues, and gets to the diamonds. If only the man in the left frame knew that he was only inches away, before he gave up. That's success in a nutshell. We are blind to the future but if we dig tenaciously today, then the future begins to become clearer with each day. YOU'RE GETTING CLOSER.

The key isn't in what you're getting right; it's staying the course when things are going wrong. Look at any single successful person in business, sports, music, etc. Understand that for every game won, tracks that made it onto to the final album cut, a person who's made their millionth dollar, have numerous failed attempts that fell short. But as the saying goes, "If you throw enough shit, some of it is bound to stick." Life will stick out its leg and trip you just as you think you're in the clear and the finish line is in sight. It's only in the midst of your setbacks that you will appreciate the gravity of your triumphs. It may take a week of rain for you to appreciate the warmth of the sunlight again.

"Many of life's failures are people who did not realize how close they were when they gave up."

– THOMAS A. EDISON

---

4. PROGRESS

A tiny step is better than no step at all. One is greater than zero in every instance of productivity. There's no way around it, one is always greater than zero. Progress, progress, progress; anything moving towards your goal or working on the best version of yourself starts with that first step and advances one day at a time. By focusing on ANY progress at all really takes the pressure off yourself, and combats the feeling of failure and the pressure to have everything at once.

Progress can even take shape in the form of criticisms, so you know how to improve moving forward. Anything is better than nothing. We've talked about falling in love with the process, and this is a driving point for that very topic as well. Like clockwork, if you love what you do and the purpose you do it for, then progress is an inevitable byproduct. Progress means everything when creating a dream. The relentless pursuit of consistent improvement is what separates the greats from the ordinary.

The wonderful thing about progress is that you don't have to hit the bullseye every single time you set out to put in some work. It's all a learning experience, and the more you do, the more you learn. The more you try, the more you will succeed.

5. PRACTICE

"Practice isn't the thing you do once you're good. It's the thing you do that makes you good."

– MALCOM GLADWELL

"But Allen Iverson said..." True, but it was because of the years, and years, and years, and years of practice it took for him to get to that very minute is what allowed him to say that. Improving the overall quality of life requires practicing honesty with yourself and practicing habits that prove to be useful to you. Don't practice because you're great, practice because want to be better. You don't practice because you're strong; you practice because you were once weak. You don't practice because you are wise, you do it because you were once foolish. You don't practice because you're fearless, you practice because you were once afraid.

Practice your craft, day in and out. Put in the hours, even when you don't want to. This is what separates the great from the good and the experts from novices. That extra hour you chose to put in shooting foul shots compared to your friend who went in early that night might make all the difference in this week's game. It is said that it takes 10,000 hours to master your craft. Anything sounds impossible if you look at that number and expect to hit it any faster than you're meant to. Start chipping away at it now. Be so good at what you do that people have no choice but to notice you. Don't let your mouth do the talking, let your work speak for itself.

6. PATIENCE

Nothing worthwhile happens overnight. The efforts put forth by you day in and out, over and over again that will produce results.

There's a reason why we always hear "Patience is a virtue." Because it's true. It's important and continually developmental. You aren't just born naturally being okay with not getting what you want when you want it. Especially in today's society, with how easily accessible everything is. It makes it unbelievably difficult to be patient when everything is at the tips of our fingers.

Instant gratification is the notorious nemesis of patience and self-confidence. If you are always used to getting things immediately, then when something meaningful and worth pursuing comes along, you may begin to feel like you're not good enough, and that there's something wrong with you for not getting it as quickly as you might have expected. This notion is blatantly incorrect and you must dispel any thoughts of wrongdoing on your behalf if you are honestly taking the necessary steps to make your happiness happen. Take a deep breath and find solace in the truth that everything that should be, will be...in time.

"My heart is at ease knowing that what is meant for me will never miss me, and that which misses me was never meant for me."

– IMAM AL-SHAFI'I

Being patient is the underlying story in any successful individual's life. If you ask them how they made things happen, I will guarantee that somewhere in that conversation, besides hard work and resilience, you're going to hear the word patience a few times.

CHAPTER 16

HOW TO BE LUCKY

Luck, in a few words, is when preparation meets opportunity. Luck looks a lot like hard work. You don't just lie on your couch wishing for something to happen and then, BOOM! Crashing through your roof comes a bag of money, your soulmate, and the master key to a happy life. Unfortunately, it just doesn't happen like that. It takes grueling tenacity working towards your dream, and then finally being in the right place at the right time. This is where all of your hard work and preparation turns into "luck" when you finally get that opportunity you've been waiting for. In the realm of taking action in a window of opportunity, seldom is there a perfect climate. There's no rain check for a missed opportunity. The show goes on with or without you.

Luck is setting yourself down the same proven path as other like-minded people before you, with you, and around you; sooner or later you're going to run into what you're seeking when the time is right, in the place it is meant to be. That's luck. The key is to commit before you're ready because if you miss an opportunity, it almost never presents itself twice. Once it's gone, it's gone and you're haunted by yet another road not taken wondering only, what if?

Luck is surrounding yourself with what you wish to attract into your life. Some of us are naïve enough to think that luck is going to strike like lightning, even if it isn't what we've been setting ourselves up for. Luck should feel less like a blindsided punch to the face, and more like a promotion; it might come as a surprise, but you knew this day would come sooner or later because it's what you've been setting yourself up for by the work you chose to put in.

Honestly, the fact that you were born and to this day draw breath in your lungs at this very moment constitutes you as lucky. Luck isn't just winning the lottery; it's being grateful for being put in the position you are currently in. Luck is being thankful for not dropping dead yesterday, being privileged with another day of life, and another opportunity to put your skills to practice in creating the life you know you deserve!

QUICK TIP

Create your own luck by constantly placing yourself in opportunities to succeed. Sign up for contests and competitions. Attend conferences and summits where networking opportunities may present themselves. Just when you think it's safe to rest is when opportunity may strike! Be ready. Be vigilant. Be willing. Be fearless. Go for it and luck will indeed be on your side. Sleep through your opportunity and see that luck fall in somebody else's lap.

CHAPTER 17

GETTING THE POISON OUT

Intimidation, inferiority complex, self-loathing and self-doubt are all forms of poison slowing you, paralyzing you, and eventually killing you; let the poison in and find yourself forever halted from reaching unrivaled heights to which your eyes are fixed upon. Rid these words and the habits that accompany them from your life forever to live happily and more successfully than you even knew possible. There's so much to be said on the topic of how to achieve success in whatever you do, but let's talk about how not to achieve it.

The poison is already in all of us. We can either decide to be the antidote or the accelerator until it slowly and painfully kills us. This psychological poison will slither its way through all of your thoughts, and over time paralyze your actions, finally ending the chance at the life you once thought was in your reach.

INTIMIDATION

It's no secret that we can feel intimidated at times, like when you're new to a job, area, or against stiff competition. Overcome it by reiterating to yourself, "I'm here for a reason" when you find yourself in these situations. Why is it that you're there against tough competition? It's because YOU are tough competition, and the person opposite of you feels the same exact angst. If you want to win in life, you cannot concern yourself with the doings of others. Put on your blinders, stay in your lane, and proceed intrepidly.

Believe you're there for a reason and that you came to win. Dedicate yourself to success. Dedicate yourself to greatness. Make it your obsession. Outwork the competition and never feel threatened by opposition...BE THE THREAT. Let nothing stand in the way of your success.

INFERIORITY COMPLEX

Eventually we're all faced with times when we look in the mirror and don't see someone as good as the next person; not for any rational reason, it's just a feeling. No facts, just your own mind planting seeds of doubt. There is nothing that another person possesses making you any less capable of turning your labor into deserved fruit. Look that person back in the mirror and tell them that they're wrong, and then prove it. You must first win the battle within your mind before setting body to purposeful action. The lack or abundance of confidence is the defining difference between failure and success. Everything means nothing without the confidence to execute. Don't say to yourself that you're great because it'll pump you up; believe that you're great because you are. Believe you're the best in the room and find other people begin to line up behind you.

SELF-LOATHING

Another self-destructive state to dwell in; it doesn't let us feel like we should be happy, and that's just unacceptable. If you aren't living up to your expectations or your actions are contrary to your intentions, you tend to sink to a place of anger with yourself. Your current situation can be changed in an instant with just a thought in the right direction. Never spend time hating who you are or what you have become. You alone are responsible for what comes next.

We place so much pressure on ourselves and overload our minds with the myth of perfectionism. You forget that you in fact do have tomorrow, and the next day, next month, and next year to work, little by little to unburden yourself from perfectionism and start working on progress vs. perfection.

The problem as humans is that we want what we want, and we want it now. The fact is that very little happens with the snap of your fingers. Hating yourself for putting so much pressure on getting it now is counterproductive to the happiness you deserve. Relax, smile, and say to yourself "Okay, if not today, then tomorrow." Eventually, one of those tomorrows will become the today you're looking for. Don't take yourself or life too seriously. Enjoy life. Enjoy yourself.

SELF-DOUBT

If you have a voice inside telling you that you CAN'T do something, then go out and do it, and then you've just silenced that voice forever. Cynicism and skepticism is the graveyard of all creativity and exploration. If the voice in your head tells you that you're going to fail before you even try, and you BELIEVE it...you're right, maybe you aren't ever going to do anything great. Belief is pivotal, not the belief in the voice of self-doubt, but the belief that you can do it, and once you have, then whoever told you that you can't is wrong. So is the voice in your head. Arnold Schwarzenegger said, "I love it when somebody says that no one has ever done this before, because then when I do it that means I am the first one that has done it. So pay no attention to the people that say it cant be done." You need to drown that negative self-doubting pestilence whispering limiting thoughts in your ear. There are no limits but the ones you place on yourself. Remove them and the world is yours. Go get it.

QUICK TIP

Finding your mind becoming infected with poison? Practice positive affirmations aloud, and write them on post-it-notes next to what meets your sightline in your living space: a mirror in the bathroom or refrigerator for example.

TUG OF WAR: HEAD VS. HEART

It feels like our heart and head are constantly pulling us in different directions. The constant struggle of the internal dialogue, and tireless tug of war between the two fighting over what is best for you and what you want. These two things might and might not be the same thing at times. It can become taxing, wrestling with the idea of appeasing both or choosing between them. This is why the suggestion of allowing them both to work in unison and bringing to light your true desire presents itself.

WHO'S RIGHT? WHO'S WRONG? BOTH. NEITHER.

Listen to your heart. It will guide you in the direction of what you desire to attract into existence, but also listen to your mind; for it will direct you toward the smartest ways to obtain what your heart desires. Our heart and mind are placed in the same body for a reason. <u>Don't ignore one in attempt to satisfy the other.</u>

It's success and happiness suicide if you always let one be in the driver's seat. There are times where we know who we have to let drive, but there needs to be a compromise. Passion and purpose is more important than anything that drives your desires, but knowing what to do and how to obtain that goal is equally as paramount.

The head and heart seem like they have a complicated relationship, and it's true, but unlucky for them, they're stuck together for life. Balance is where you will find the result each one is looking for. Like any relationship, one person will think they're right. They will fight, but at the end of the day, come to understand each other. Your mind will try to overthink, worry, and rationalize everything to the point you won't want to even do it anymore. Your heart will say go, go, go, having no regard for what comes next. Find what balances the scale to find happiness and success in everything you do.

Never underestimate the tendency of human beings to act contrary to their best interests. Human behavior (most of the time) works like this; act then learn, when in some important cases we should learn then act. What's best for us? Who's to say? Some people are better at learning from consequences, experiences, and letting their heart lead them into the depths of the unknown and others, from their preparation leading up to an action. Balance is the key to everything in life. The combination of preparation and risk is a recipe for conscious decisions yielding positive results in the favor of what you know you want. The downward spiral of decision-making disasters stems from acting against our best interests, denying our heart to lead us to passion and ignoring what the rationale for it is.

Acting against our best interests and creating empty satisfaction stems from constantly seeking instant gratification from fleeting pleasures, instead of following meaningful pursuits when it counts.

QUICK TIP

Remind yourself of why it's something you want. Does it play into your picture of happiness or will it add to what "makes sense" in your life at the expense of it?

CHAPTER 19

ONE ON ONE WITH ADVERSITY

In the dressing room, the lights are dimmed, you've tuned out the noise, and for this moment you are alone with your thoughts just minutes before your fight. "Jab, jab, cross, bob; jab, jab, weave. Stick and move, stick and move. Feel them out, dance around the ring, control the pace, be first, circle away from their power hand, mind your breathing, and make them fight your fight. You got this." Your name is called, walkout song echoing throughout the arena, you were nervous, but not anymore: calm, focused, a dormant volcano on the cusp of a monumental eruption.

Ding! Ding! Ding! You shuffle across the ring; your opponent is in reach; your jab is followed by nothing but a cool breeze. A half-second later, BOOM! Your opponent slipped your jab and hit you with a straight right hand you never saw coming. Hitting the canvas, down for the count, before you landed a single shot, thinking to yourself, "Wow, this isn't the way it was supposed to go."

Now What? Practice all you want, but you'll know exactly what you're made of and what you're going to do next. In that very instant you take an unanticipated punch to the face that sends you to the canvas like a sack of potatoes. You're introduced to your true nature and learn the most about yourself in the face of adversity. Anybody can smile when they're up, but when you're in the gutter, beaten, and downtrodden, what version of yourself will you be introduced to?

"It is not the critic who counts; not the man who points out how the strong man stumbles, or where the doer of deeds could have done them better. The credit belongs to the man who is actually in the arena, whose face is marred by dust and sweat and blood; who strives valiantly; who errs, who comes short again and again, because there is no effort without error and shortcoming; but who does actually strive to do the deeds; who knows great enthusiasms, the great devotions; who spends himself in a worthy cause; who at the best knows in the end the triumph of high achievement, and who at the worst, if he fails, at least fails while daring greatly, so that his place shall never be with those cold and timid souls who neither know victory nor defeat. "*

– THEODORE ROOSEVELT
THE MAN IN THE ARENA.

No one gets to where they're going in life unscathed. You will earn scars, seen and unseen. You will make plans and they will be interrupted. You will know everything and then you will know nothing. Anything can happen in a moment, your life changed in an instant. Expect the unexpected. Easy to say, hard to do. How can we expect the unexpected, if we're not expecting it? Good question. The constant stop and start of life is what keeps you on your toes. Life happens, and it always will. Knowledge of this truth is the closest thing we can get to counter punching life.

Things are tough, but never impossible. A positive mindset changes everything. Simply realize that obstacles are really opportunities in disguise. Turn a mess into a miracle. Take these opportunities as a chance to prove that each day you are better than the last, and one step closer to conquering your goals. With hard work and perseverance, nothing is out of reach.

THE FIGHT IS WON IN THE GYM

"The fight is won or lost far away from witnesses – behind the lines, in the gym, and out there on the road, long before I dance under those lights"

– MUHAMMAD ALI

The fight with adversity is won in the mind even before going toe-to-toe out in the real world. You've got to establish a strong footing, grounded in the confidence of your actions and intuition. Your foundation must be solid. Before a punch is thrown, it must carry itself though the kinetic chain, starting from the ground up, and out whipping with speed and deadly intent. Your mindset is the foundation of all actions that follow and the success or lack thereof soon after. Trust yourself and you will be guided onto the proper path.

There are no dead ends in life. There is always a way out, around, and through times of strife. Contrary to popular belief, there are always options, despite what lies in front of you. First, take a step back to open the up the mind to a rational, realistic approach to the situation. Next, a positive perspective to assist in the realization that you aren't trapped; it's merely just a stress response that you're feeling.

Finally, gather the confidence and courage to approach the solution to do what is necessary for yourself, and ultimately is best for your happiness.

A lie they tell you is that, "It's not that simple." False. It is that simple. Make up your mind and do what they told you wasn't possible or isn't going to be as simple as you think it will. This is what they tell you to keep you down. The truth is, with a mind certain of success with the assistance of unrelenting willpower, everything becomes simple because in your mind, there's only one option: success.

A LETTER TO ADVERSITY

Dear Adversity,

I dare you. I dare you to test me. I dare you to try me. I dare you to threaten my success. I dare you. You will watch me win. You will feel me conquer you. You will see me rise to the occasion. You will see me destroy you, then the goals thereafter, and the ones after that.

I say again, I dare you to stand in my way. Move or be moved. Those are your options. You are transparent. I see through you, beyond you, and the victory that lies behind you. It's nothing personal, but you will be defeated in the pursuit of my greatness. I will fight as though I have trekked through a barren desert, parched, a day from death, and behind you? There lies a crystal-clear, frigid stream that flows with liquid vitality.

Finally, I say once more, it's not personal, you see, its survival. I must advance. I must succeed. The way I see it is you will lose or I will die. I commend you for your courage, but now I must seize what is mine.

Sincerely,

....

Sign in the space provided above

CHAPTER 21

PROCRASTINATION AND PRODUCTIVITY, FRIENEMIES?

" You call it procrastination. I call it thinking. "

– AARON SORKIN

Procrastination is productivity's arch nemesis. Or maybe they're putting on a front for the public eye, and really hang out in their spare time because they have a lot in common ...but still somewhat hate each other.

TAKE FIVE

If you currently are a generally productive person, if you're trying to be a productive person, or whether you're a dancer trying to get down some really tedious choreography, but can't seem to remember the steps after practicing all day and all through the night, it's not because you're dumb. It's not because you've failed. You might just need a break. Go and take five.

Here's why doing something else and putting it off until tomorrow might help you more than you think:

1. The Zeigarnik Effect is when people remember incomplete or interrupted tasks better than completed ones. The idea is, that once you've completed a task, it is easily forgotten because there is no longer a need to remember it, thrown into a preverbal forgotten filing cabinet. This can be the missing link in perfecting your personal productivity hacks. Sometimes picking up another unrelated activity in the meantime or taking a walk can make all the difference in firing on all cylinders the next time you pick up your original project.

2. The Ovsiankina Effect, circles around the same idea. It refers to one picking a task back up at the earliest opportunity. A sudden stop or cease-fire to reframe our focus can jump-start our productivity. Focus can be lost, even when you think you're paying attention, coasting through rather than devoting full attention. It often takes a quick full stop to restart your mind's focus on the task. For example, when a teacher, during a lecture, notices his or her students' focus fading, they might say, "Everybody stand up! Stretch and sit back down." This is similar to listening to loud music. After a while, you won't really notice the volume as you would if you were someone with fresh ears walking into the room. If someone presses pause, immediately your mind says, where'd the music go? When it resumes, you now have to adjust your focus back to the previous level.

FIND WHAT WORKS FOR YOU

There are all different kinds of people in the world when it comes to the methods of their productivity, and that's perfectly fine. Allowing things to evolve into what they want to be, rather than forcing something unnaturally is what we're ultimately looking for. Whatever it takes to foster your pure intention to create is what's important; doing it right over rushing its completion. If that means picking it up later, then so be it.

There's nothing worse than forcing a thing to be something it's not. This works with everything in life, in relationships, jobs, art, writing, school, friendships, etc. There's no damage done in taking breaks, trying something new, or coming back to a task when the light bulb above your head finally clicks on and the task shapes into what it needs to be.

Aaron Sorkin said, "You call it procrastination. I call it thinking." Yes, waiting until the last minute, then cramming in all of your effort is the death of creativity and productivity. But! If you find the sweet spot in between rushing straight away to finish and finishing last-minute, that's where lightning strikes. It then potentially becomes a perfect balance of creativity and productivity. Leaving a task incomplete for the time being, and coming back to it later suggests striking the perfect balance in molding and sharpening your task.

Think about it. Every day we're learning and processing new information. The person who worked on that certain project isn't the same one working on it today. Every day you become a little better at shaping your skill set and fluid in your thinking. A fresh look may allow your mind to transform your work into something better than you ever knew it had the potential to be when you first started it.

Different personalities require different methods, but if you do find yourself procrastinating, do it productively.

SECTION TWO
TRANSFORM

CHAPTER 22

MAGIC MOMENT

"I'm happy and this is exactly where I want to be. If I could, I wouldn't change a thing." Can you look in the mirror and sincerely say this about your own life right now?

If not, that's okay! Just make a change. Whatever you think, feel, and say is what you attract into your life. If you wish for more, then become more. Make intelligent decisions and positive changes to get yourself where you see you need to be. You possess all of the tools necessary to create the life that you want. Wholeheartedly believe that you do not exist to merely dredge through the mundane motions of feeling like you need to settle for anything less than what you deserve. YOU are the only one who has the power over your life to mold it into something amazing, and to be proud of. Start NOW because it is the youngest you will ever be.

TAKE THE PLUNGE

The most terrifying part about making change is much like jumping into a pool and finding the initial shock of jumping in., even though moments after taking the plunge you know you'll be okay. It's the moment leading up to that state change that is fearful, but ultimately is just that, a state change from this to that. Listen to the voice in your heart that tells you to do it and ignore the ones telling you not to. More importantly, listen to the voice and recognize the moments that inch you closer toward the edge, ready to jump. Don't ignore the signs that you need a change. Sometimes signs may not appear as an obvious "Wrong way" as you enter the exit ramp, but a simple question to provoke a thought. Instead of asking yourself, "Has it gotten this bad that I need a change?" ask, "Is this good enough for me to remain the same?"

TEN YEARS AND OVERNIGHT IS THE SAME THING.

If someone says, "It took me ten years to change that," or, "for me it happened overnight." Guess what, it happened for both of these people in one single moment. Anyone who wanted to change something major in his or her life can trace it back to that one singular moment of realization. Maybe the moment you decided to start eating healthy, the moment you threw yourself all-in with your business, the moment you chose happiness over being miserable, or the moment you decided to let go and move on. All of them have that one moment in common and the path that got you there.

The person who said it took them ten years is correct. It may have taken them ten years to work at what they desired when they finally became honest with themselves in that single defining moment. There was a similar defining moment as well for the person who claimed it happened overnight. It all boils down to the moment you became real enough with yourself to recognize the problem, and start working on the solution. I can't tell you what that problem or solution is, the only person that can is you.

The first step to a magic moment is looking in the mirror, admitting you need a change, and then commit to making it. Lasting life-changing moments require a strength that you might not have known you had. It will be uncomfortable, but didn't comfort and fear get you here to this moment of change? Here's the great thing, these moments are unlimited; you can have as many moments as you need to create the person you know you have the potential to be.

QUICK TIPS

1. You Have to Want it: You can't be forced into making a change or you will more than likely find an excuse to slither your way out of it.

2. Rid Negativity: Reframe your mindset for positivity in every aspect of every day. Expel whatever negative thoughts, habits, and people you have to from your life.

3. Build a Support Network: Surround yourself with likeminded people and those who aim to guide you toward new beginnings.

4. Eliminate Non-essentials: Only take with you mentally and physically what you need to focus on your transformation. Everything else is just extra.

5. Baby Steps: Any step forward is progress, no matter the size.

6. Change to Be Free: Never change to become someone else. Change to break your true identity free.

CHAPTER 23

BREAK PATTERNS.
CREATE HABITS.

The road to acquiring different results takes drastic and immediate action. Wishing to evolve from your current emotional, physical, occupational situation requires a shift into a new direction. The key to creating new habits is to unravel current ones by redesigning the way you achieve your goal. Everything begins to look the same when you're floating in familiarity. What was once shiny is now lackluster and forgetful. Routine interruption can unlock the dormant eruption of energy to reach your destination in a new and interesting way. Change: you realize you have to make one, but how?

BREAKING PATTERNS

1. Do something different.

Starting tomorrow, do something different that shakes up your whole day. Engage in something that makes you feel differently. If you think about it right now, you probably know almost exactly what each day will be. You watch your shows on Sunday, Monday is work and pasta night, Tuesdays you read a book, etc.

The first step to anything change-oriented is to simply do something different. Create the change you wish to see. Predetermined days are accompanied by predetermined thought and action patterns. Mix it up.

2. Plan to do something you've been meaning to do but never got around to.

There's nothing that fuels procrastination more than a goal set too far into the future. You find yourself doing a million other things and falling into a groove that's now impossible to get out of, pushing that desirable task further and further into non-existence. Stop doing that. Specifically, set a day this week, take off of work, cancel a prior plan, do whatever you have to do to make it happen. It's going to be hard to bail if you've canceled all of your routine distractions. Remember if you really want something bad enough you will make time, not excuses.

CREATING HABITS

1. Start Intrinsically: Have a strong purpose as to why you need to make this change. Find the motivation that keeps you going.

2. "If-Then": Your goal to become healthier. So, instead of choosing random instances sprinkled into your day, try to plan such activities. For example, IF it is time to eat lunch, THEN make it healthy. IF you just got home from work, change your clothes, and THEN go to the gym. Make links between your time and your activities.

3. Convenience: The textbook excuse to give us when we abandon a promise to ourselves is that it was out of our way or you didn't have the time to do it. Eliminate this notion by tailoring your current life to the one you wish to live. For example, if you plan to go to the gym every day, before you go to sleep, pick out your gym clothes and place them on top of your dresser or TV (if there is one in your room). It's easy to find your excuse to skip the gym if you're lying in bed watching TV, and your gym clothes are in the other room; not easy if they're blocking your TV or right next to you.

4. Set Micro-Goals: Think about the bare minimum that you MUST do each and every day with the big picture in mind. If drinking more water is your goal, then pick up a Gallon jug to refill. Every day mark off the amount you must drink by certain times of the day, and do it. Find these micro goals within every area you wish to improve, and see yourself to the certainty of success.

CHALLENGE

Seriously devote the rest of this entire week toward completing all of the above. Start with why. Know the purpose of your change. Why is it important to you? Start there. Next, do something different. Do what you've put off for a while now. Make your change convenient for your life. Set your micro goals every morning, starting tomorrow. Go!

CHAPTER 24

BE LIKE WATER

"Be like water making its way through cracks. Do not be assertive, but adjust to the object, and you shall find a way around or through it. If nothing within you stays rigid, outward things will disclose themselves. Empty your mind, be formless. Shapeless, like water. If you put water into a cup, it becomes the cup. You put water into a bottle and it becomes the bottle. You put it in a teapot, it becomes the teapot. Now, water can flow or it can crash. Be water, my friend."

– BRUCE LEE

Practice patience and adaptability through and flow freely with the moments of your ever-changing life. Those two words will help you smoothly navigate through choppy waters. Stay the course. Free your mind and "be like water."

OPPORTUNITY IS SNEAKY

Opportunity won't "jump" out at you. The word presents itself in various ways throughout our lives. Sometimes it will be as bold as a neon "open" sign with blinking arrows pointing to it, and other times it'll be as subtle as a cool summer's breeze. It happens when you least expect it...which is more common. It's ironic, because opportunity doesn't always present itself at the most opportune times. It happens when you won't be ready, but have to be, so adapt accordingly.

Preparation is key. Expect nothing but be prepared for everything. More often than not, what you set out to do in the beginning will not be what you end up doing in the end. Our life can change in an instant, and so can our desires. It's okay to open up to new possibilities and find out where they lead you. It doesn't mean you've done all your previous work for nothing, it means that everything you've done thus far has led you right here and now, no matter how winding the road.

DON'T BE ONE OF "THOSE PEOPLE"

Those who speak with regret are the ones who never opened up their mind to possibility and remained within their comfort zone. They speak from a place of disappointment, often not in what they did, but what they didn't do. They always thought "inside the box," when in reality, there is no "box"; life is what you choose to make it and comes in whatever shape you choose to confine yourself to or free yourself from. They are blinded by what they "think they're supposed to be doing," when at any time something else can come along and change your entire life. Don't be one of those people.

Authentic, shadow-casting regret is different than the consequences of gambling with your choices. It comes from recognizing your desires, seeing the opportunity, and proceeding to do nothing. Make each your own, and leave as little to chance as possible. Do not stifle adventure presented by a possibility. Your life is the sum of your choices as much as it is your thoughts. Choose wisely, but be true to yourself. Never change for anyone but you, especially not for public appearances or for the satisfaction of others. Each and every one of us is entitled to live our lives dictated by only ourselves. Opening your mind and accepting opportunity with open arms may lead to the life you've always dreamed of, without even looking for it. In the end, it's never about what you seek, but what is actually seeking you.

ADAPTATION IS NOW YOUR BASELINE

The key to living an exceptional life and achieving maximum performance is not only to adapt to change, but to thrive in its wake. Adaptation to creating life-changing circumstances as you seek improvement is crucial, but only the beginning.

Your adaptation is the new baseline. After each level of mastery, you then find yourself having to adapt after your previous achievement level. It's easy to view change when there is a predetermined structure to it. In our own lives, since it pushes and pulls us in every direction, it springs on us rather quickly and there isn't a rulebook in the world that can tell me how to achieve a result the same way you do. There are levels to excellence and development. With each stage comes self-discovery and exciting exploration.

CHAPTER 25

LET GROW AND LET GO

With every day, month, and year of our lives that we are privileged enough to draw breath in, we grow and evolve and find something new within the world that strikes us with a sense of wonder, undiscovered by our former selves. We were all someone else yesterday, and will become someone new tomorrow. Allow life to show you who that person is and what sensations they'll discover. With each heartbeat comes the unveiling of intricacies unseen, unfelt, and not yet lived.

Before you wish to be trapped at an age or could go back to a "better" time, remember you're depriving your future self of the life yet discovered. Everything happened for a reason and acceptance is important if you intend to have a brighter tomorrow without a dark cloud passing over your sun every twenty minutes.

LET GROW

Everybody wants a quick fix or an elevator straight to the top. People want a diet pill but don't want to eat right or workout. They want an overnight business plan to make a million dollars but don't want to actually have to work for it. Everyone is looking for their chance to hit their personal lottery. But you don't, you know what it takes or you wouldn't be here. Your life reflects what you repeatedly do every day. If you develop good habits, then good things will follow. The same applies in the opposite direction.

There's no secret to living the life you want, and the answers aren't all found in one place. Exploration of your talents, and practicing positive habits is a better start than hoping someone develops a "Happy and Fulfilled Life" pill that will never come to exist.

Plant the seed of thought and water it every day with your attitude and actions. The amount of time that is takes to form a new habit is a rain drop in the ocean compared to the growth it produces for the rest of your days. This sounds like enough time to start a beautiful life, one thought, one action, and one habit at a time. What do you think?

LET GO

One of the harder things to do is to let go. Putting an end to what you're used to is difficult. It's also what made you need change. Letting go of your fears, letting go of what's holding you back, letting go of unhealthy attachments for the greater good; holding on can hurt you more in the long run a lot more than letting go.

Leave behind what you need to in order to move on. If you do this for the right reasons, then you may find yourself in a new situation that you only once dreamed of. Stagnant water is never healthy to drink, so why let your life become the same way? Allow water to descend freely from the mountaintop, providing fresh, healthy water to flow outward from your mind and into your life. It all starts in the mind and flows outward.

5 THINGS TO LET GO RIGHT NOW...

1. Trying to Please Everyone: Remember, your happiness matters too. You can't please everyone. Make yourself your top priority.

2. Living in the Past: You've already been there, and it's not going to change, but tomorrow can. Turn the past into a memory and not a refuge from the uncertainty of tomorrow's greatness.

3. Fearing Change: For all the caterpillar knows, its cocoon might be a coffin, right? We all know what happens next.

4. Overthinking: Don't think long enough to create problems that aren't there.

5. Putting Yourself Down: Life knocks you down enough. The least you can do is give yourself a hand back up.

 REMEMBER

You can't change where you've been but you can change where you're going. It all starts with one thought and two words: "what if." After you've got that down, the possibilities are endless. Just write down those two words and fill in the rest.

CHAPTER 26

A BRAND NEW YOU

Try New Things! Meet New People! Travel to New Places!

Life is too short and filled with too many pleasures not to take advantage of it at every opportunity. Seize the moment, for it will only last the duration it takes for you to utter, "Yes" or "No." I dare you to say YES! Take a step into the unknown, get lost in an adventure. You may like what you find. Life is a journey paved and unpaved with endless, beautiful experiences just waiting for you to stumble upon. Approach each endeavor with a positive attitude and an open mind. Don't stop until you have written a story that you could only dream of telling.

Have you been suppressing your true nature? Have you lost yourself to an unfavorable routine? Are you unhappy with where things have ended up thus far? Whatever your moment of enlightenment was, you're already better off for having recognized it! Now, it's time you found out who you are in light of your recognition of a life-pivoting change. Start with experimenting and engaging in a life unfamiliar to you. See what these new adventures will bring out in you. Welcome with open arms something new and embrace what it brings.

TRY NEW THINGS

The old you dies every night and reborn anew every morning. Who will you be today? What will you try today that you were curious about yesterday? Humans are creatures of habit, and variety is what keeps things interesting. Shake it up a bit. Doesn't it give you a flicker of excitement when you think about throwing something new into the mix? New is scary. New is riveting. New is curious. New is necessary.

Whether it's a dash per year or a daily practice, you deserve the feeling of pleasant surprises sprinkled into your life. Submit to an experience that you are afraid to try and stop making excuses for why NOT to do things. Allow life to take you by the hand and lead you on an adventure you could only wish for in your wildest dreams.

MEET NEW PEOPLE

Frequently place yourself in situations where you're meeting and interacting with new people. Instead of going to this coffee shop today, go to that one. Instead of going your normal spot this weekend, go to that one. Waiting in line? Start a conversation. See someone reading the same book as you? Talk about it. Life's too short and bountiful to never take the opportunity to share in the connection with someone new. Even use it as an excuse for a self-development exercise. If you're shy, this is a perfect opportunity to challenge yourself. Go to places where you know you'll never meet those people again, and start a conversation with at least one person. Share stories, thoughts, or concerns. Share a piece you yourself and absorb a piece of them. We all cross paths for a reason, so stick around for a second to find out why.

TRAVEL TO NEW PLACES

The world is bigger than your street. Get out there and see it! Think of anywhere you've ever wanted to go, then go! Ideally, a teleportation device would come in handy because the reality is that life calls for our responsibility to our duties within it. Not everyone can get up and go, just like that. Although, what's more than possible right now is to put an immediate end to saying you **wish** blank, and you **want** to blank, and **you've always thought about** going to blank. Make goals, not excuses. Devise a plan to get there as soon as your life allows it. Take the first step toward that plan starting tomorrow.

CHAPTER 27

BURN THE BOATS

"A long while ago, a great warrior faced a situation which made it necessary for him to make a decision which insured his success on the battlefield. He was about to send his armies against a powerful foe, whose men outnumbered his own. He loaded his soldiers into boats, sailed to the enemy's country, unloaded soldiers and equipment, then gave the order to burn the ships that had carried them. Addressing his men before the first battle, he said, "You see the boats going up in smoke. That means that we cannot leave these shores alive unless we win! We now have no choice—we win, or we perish! They won."

– NAPOLEON HILL, THINK AND GROW RICH

What do you desire most of all? Is it success, change, happiness, satisfaction, fulfillment, or all of the above? Whatever your answer, here's how to get it: Burn The Boats.

"BOATS" DEFINED

If you have no choice but to win, you will. It's as simple as that. Forcing yourself into an instinctual sense of survival means it's kill or be killed, win or lose. If there is no chance of retreat, you better believe you're going to get to where you need to go. Boats are anything in your life that is holding you back from fully and truly going all-in to commit to your dream. It's whatever scares you to let go of in case of failure. It's time to ditch the safety net. Your boats are what keep you one foot in and one foot out of the door; you're never really committed when you have so many fallbacks. These can be a physical or psychological stimuli holding you back. The key is the realization of what it is first and then dealing with its incineration.

An expired relationship, a dead end job, the fear of stepping out of your comfort zone, afraid to put yourself out of the line? There are various boats for different people. Find what impedes your success. Only then will you understand the urgency to win, because now you don't have a choice.

BOATS BURNED, STARING AT A PILE OF ASH... WHAT NOW?

Once you have cut ties with everything that scares you back to "reality," we will only then truly feel free to fight for what you deserve: whatever occupies your wildest dreams. Your reality is whatever you make it, and is shaped by what you think. Your thoughts are the foundation of what your life is built on. Reality is only a term made to frighten us into social norms that are acceptable within the parameters of what society suggests your life should be. Sometimes we forget that we don't HAVE to do anything. It's often the things we think we're supposed to be doing that hold us back the most.

Set sail; allow your mind to reach your destination. It's time to break out your matches, so strike, burn, and walk forward, smiling as you stroll briskly into a brighter tomorrow. There's no turning back. No retreat. No surrender. Victory will be yours!

CHALLENGE

Take some time to sit down on a selected day to audit your life. Sit down and be honest with where you are and where you want to be. If that doesn't involve where you currently are right now, then by God, start burning some boats. Write down everything that you feel is holding you back. Let it flow from your heart and out through your pen: emotions, thoughts, people, a mindset, anything and everything that anchors you, paralyzed in a state of uncertainty. Look at that paper. Look at all that you have identified in that short amount of time. Now burn it. Release yourself.

CHAPTER 28

HOW TO STOP DOING THINGS YOU HATE

Summary in a sentence: Stop doing it.

Stop doing things you hate! As soon as you stop doing things you don't want to do, that's where your life begins to really make a U-turn. Put a cease to unfavorable habits draining your time and energy. Unfortunately, you can't slide into magic ruby slippers, click your heels three times, and teleport yourself to where you wish to be. The good news is that you can wear any kind of shoes you want and be exactly where you want to be...in time. It's called, make an initial positive change in the right direction, right now, and begin walking.

> *"Whatever excites you, go do it.*
> *Whatever drains you, stop doing it."*
>
> – DEREK SIVERS

The straight line to a happier, purposeful life starts with doing what excites you and stopping what drains you. Trust yourself and where your energy takes you. Allow nothing to stifle your enthusiasm! There is always room for a change in where you place your energy. There is just about nothing you **must** do; however, there is always a choice.

Consequences? Yes, but there is always a choice. That choice, every single time should be to abandon all that drains you and cling to what gives you life.

Take a look at the things you hate doing and ask yourself if in any way, shape, or form it's going to help get you to where you want to go. There's no sense in doing things you hate if they lead to dead ends. Why drive a hundred miles in the wrong direction when you could have used a GPS, map, or even a pit stop to ask somebody for a point in the right direction.

You want your hard work to pay off right? You want that promotion? You want to build something of your own? You want to be happy? You want to be healthier? You want to start living your dream? Is what you're doing everyday helping you get there? Is your current way of life leading you to desired end? If they're not, then that's your starting point.

Deeply feel and hear what your mind and body are saying to you every day. Stop wasting time and energy on things that aren't a part of the bigger picture in your life. If what you're doing today isn't birthing or nurturing to exuberant health the dream you have, then stop doing it, because it's as good as murder. You're slowly adding to the death sentence of your happiness and your ideal future. You're killing what calls to you every second you do something contrary to answering it. Stop standing in your own way.

Maybe our dreams aren't created as much as they are bestowed. You have skills, traits, interests, and amazing gifts that will attract into your life what genuinely fills you with purpose. The thing that wants you the most is a received call, not outgoing. Make sure you pick up. Every day you spend feeding into the negativity of things you wish you could change, your dreams and aspirations are slipping through your fingers like sand in an hourglass. Will you have enough sand left to build what you want, or will you only be left with a few grains turned empty void, a vague fading remembrance of what could have been?

CHALLENGE

This week work to eliminate something that wastes your time, doesn't add value to your day, and misplaces your energy. Think of one thing that excites you, seems interesting to try, and start doing that in its place. It could be any negative habit or activity. Replace it with one that comes from a place of joy.

STOP WHINING AND START WINNING

Anyone can complain. It takes a courageous and committed person to take life-altering action and do something about it to actually make the change. In case you just glanced at the sentence above, it takes a COURAGEOUS and COMMITTED person to change direction that's attracting them to want more for their life.

Making life-changing actions for the better, while for the better, are rarely easier. You can complain about it, but what are you actually doing about it? Below you will find a test to separate your complaints into two categories. This will save you both time and effort in two seconds or less. It consists of one question and two possible answers:

BEGIN TEST.

1. Can you do anything about it?

A. YES

B. NO

Directions: If you answered YES: do something about it.

If you answered NO: accept it and move on.

END TEST.

Sometimes we spend wasteful amounts of time worrying about changing things that we have no control over, when all we needed to do was ask ourselves honestly if we can really do anything about it. In life there are things that we will never have control over, and that's okay. Accepting is the hard part, but it easier once we identify the things in our life that are changeable and those that are not. If you have control over it, and can do something about it, then do it! Take this test every time you hear yourself complaining. Complaining about the uncontrollable is a treadmill taking you absolutely nowhere. Negativity such as this only reproduces at alarming rates, breeding more negativity.

IF YOU CAN, YOU MUST.

What is something in life that gives us a sense of comfort? It's the fact that we know we have control over certain things within it. You can certainly control the outcome of changeable circumstances. Really sink your teeth into what you CAN do something about. Be brave enough to take action, spend the time and effort tenaciously fighting for a positive change in your life if what you hate doing is changeable.

IF YOU CAN'T, DON'T SWEAT IT.

Just the opposite applies for the things you CAN'T change. Let these things be a memory, a passing wind. Never give more energy than these things deserve. Accepting and advancing onto your next move is the best and only course of action that will further you into your desired direction. The problem arises when you take the test, fill in A, and then don't do anything about it. Complaining about something you have absolute control over, and failing to take responsibility for falls under the category of an excuse for your inability to change. Not a reason.

QUICK TIPS TO QUIT COMPLAINING

1. Practice a positive perspective. Stop negativity before it starts. Attitude is everything.

2. Adapt rather than resist. Swim with the current. Don't fight it. Accept life as a challenge, an opportunity to grow, rather than impossible obstacles.

3. Always move forward. In your mind and in your actions, always move forward.

4. Be thankful. Express gratitude daily to potentially bring much needed attention to how trivial what you're complaining about is.

5. Judge less. If your complaints are about someone else's life, then stop judging them according to your standards. Live and let live.

CHAPTER 30

WEATHERING THE STORM

The eye of the storm is the calm in the middle of chaos, standing unscathed. Serenity found in the middle, in the violence of an unrelenting storm, peace. A quiet reminder of who we are in the midst of the whipping winds and roaring thunder that surrounds us.

Adapting to change can be difficult. You may feel more like a kite dancing in a hurricane rather than a skilled sailor on the smoothest sea. It's confusing. It's difficult. It will force you to grow or perish. It throws you in directions unfamiliar to you with only a moment to decide what comes next. A monumental life change, wanted or surprising, can shake up the understanding of the world you once knew. The one unchanging circumstance among that hurricane is who you are at your core, and having that awareness of one's self enough to remain unbeaten and unwavering within the turbulence. Upholding the mental fortitude and self-confidence is what matters most to create whatever change is needed to shift your life into a direction deserving of you. This is your moment to shine and use this change as an accelerator into the desired vision for your life.

A person who acts with valor, integrity, and unwavering will in the face of challenge is rival to no other. You become impossible to defeat in anything you choose to set your mind to. Become unbeatable in your life. Become the master of your world. Find out who you are in the thick of the times that will try your soul. Feel it down to the marrow in your bones, and even further into the core of your very being. Become the champion of your life. Adapt and evolve with times that will call upon the depths of your humanity.

Don't find yourself swept away in the wind. Ground yourself. Take solace in your position as a strong, self-aware individual emerging from the storm, rising once more to unrivaled heights. Remember that everything comes to pass. For better or for worse, you will prevail and who comes out on the other end of that storm is the decision you have to make.

SECTION THREE
MINDFUL HAPPINESS

CHAPTER 31

ALL COMES FROM WITHIN THE MIND

"All that we are is a result of what we have thought"

– BUDDHA

The human mind is the most unique and powerful gift given to each and every one of us. Our minds can imagine, create, build, destroy, process, and lead us to places we've only dreamed about, only if it is open. An open mind leads to a wide-open life of vast and endless possibility. Not an ounce of juice can be squeezed from the fruit that life has to offer with a mind any less than open.

CHANGE YOUR MIND

Whatever occupies your thoughts and dwells in your mind will manifest in your life. If your beliefs match what you've always believed, then you will go on to act the same as you always have. These actions will produce the same results as they always have, bringing you right back where you started: running on that treadmill forever in the same place. It all begins with what you believe and moves outward in your actions, rooted in your thoughts. In order to produce anything other than what you have in the past, you need only to change your mind. Shift your thoughts into the direction of your desire and everything moving outward into the world will follow suit. It starts in your mind. Change your mindset. Change your life.

YOUR MIND MUST ARRIVE FIRST

Your mind has to arrive at your destination before your life does. One does not rise to become a champion in their life, and come to master everything within it without first arriving at their desired destination in the mind before setting upon the path necessary to achieve it. All senses must be present in your mind while envisioning your ideal life. You need to see it, smell it, taste it, feel it, and hear it. Dwell in the present moment as if you're already there. If "seeing is believing," then see yourself where you want to be and believe it!

BECOME ONE WITH YOUR THOUGHTS

Your journey to your ideal life begins within. If you haven't already, start taking the time each day to practice mindfulness and mindset skills. Visualize where you want to be and exactly what it is that you desire. Feel yourself actually achieving it, crossing that finish line. With each soothing deep inhale and exhale, take in positive energy while expelling the negative. Become mindful of what you wish to bring into your life and see it manifest before you. Take time each day to be with yourself and really get in touch with where you are and where you want to be. Allow yourself to be completely immersed in your thoughts and emotions. Bathe in the sanctity of the silence. Being alone is different from being lonely. Self-discovery is the foundation of a genuinely happy life. Controlling the thoughts that drive your days is the key to finding any kind of satisfaction within your life and ultimately controlling your destiny.

STOP THINKING "REALISTICALLY"

How many times have you done something you never thought you would be able to? As humans, we never cease to surprise ourselves. The problem lies in the mindset of things becoming unreachable and "unrealistic." There's a difference between realistic and rational thoughts. Realistic thinking is a decision made in your current state, which is an alternative for saying to yourself that you're willing to settle for less, driven by motivators like the fear of failure, change, or dreaming too big and never reaching it. Don't be afraid to play the "what if..." game, as long as it fuels a positive mindset for future possibilities, rather than asking, what if I can't? What if I fail? Take your mind outside the box of realism, ascending into the realm of WHAT IF, I CAN, and I WILL.

"Being realistic is the most commonly traveled route to mediocrity."

– WILL SMITH

DECIDE WHAT COMES NEXT

The thought at the origin of a sensation is what will happen next whether you want it to or not. You will attract into your life whatever you believe comes next. Start thinking positively to breed desired results.

QUICK EXERCISE

Close your eyes and breathe deeply. Let your senses take over. Be in the now. Tune out the distractions of the world around you, and be with yourself on your own frequency in an environment most peaceful to you.

Do not focus on negative thoughts. Do not let stress and anxiety creep into your nirvana. Think of something beautiful, like an image, a memory, a destination, a sound, a smell, and then bask in it until you have found tranquility in the moment.

Finally, open your eyes and continue with your day, refreshed in both body and mind.

CHALLENGE

5 minutes per day: perform the exercise above. Do this now, no time like the present.

CHAPTER 32

CHOOSE THE TOMORROW YOU ARE GOING TO HAVE

Everything in life comes down to the way you look at it. How you choose to see what's in front of you will determine the world you are surrounded by.

Things happen, both good and bad. Sometimes there's no rationale for why negative circumstances arise. It may just be the culmination of unfavorable instances converging at that particular moment in time. We do, however, have absolute control over what happens next. The answer doesn't lay in the outcome, but rather in your perception of the present. It's imperative that you take things for how they are presented, not how you wish them to be.

Always, always, ALWAYS maintain positivity throughout the good times, and more importantly, the bad. "Good" or "Bad" days all start off the same and can sway whichever way you make it. The power is in the perception, not the situation.

Perspective is one of the most powerful tools we have in deciding our fate, and every day we have a chance to use it. Every day can be made what we want it to be. Life is filled with different plots, scenes, and characters; the only constant throughout it is you and how you perceive it.

Get excited for tomorrow starting with tonight. Turn anxiety into excitement. Don't let your head play games with you. Tomorrow is yours to take, crush each task with enthusiasm. It's "Carpe diem," not the other way around. Wake up each day and dictate how it will go.

Wake up radiating positivity into the world. Today is a new beginning! Choose to be happy the minute you open your eyes. Take time to appreciate the little things throughout your day and before the day ends, make sure to be the reason for someone else's smile.

Do these four things every single day:

1. Smile: Do it just because. Smile at yourself in the mirror. Smile at a stranger. You're alive! Embrace the miracle.

2. Make eye contact when talking to other: Establish a connection. Listen to understand, not only to respond.

3. Don't sweat the small stuff. Use the 5 by 5 rule: If it isn't going to matter in 5 years, then don't spend more than 5 minutes being bothered by it.

4. Choose to see the good in everything: always find a silver lining, no matter how small.

CHAPTER 33

IT IS WHAT IT IS

LET IT BE

It is what it is, but will be whatever you make of it. The path to a happier life is allowing each situation to be what it is, rather than what we think it should be. Make the best of every circumstance from that moment forward. Just decide to do so, and it shall begin to naturally flow like an instinct. Yes, stress exists. Yes, life is hard. Yes, life can be unfair. It doesn't mean we have to place the burden on our shoulders and worry about unchangeable events all day and night until it torments you into physical illness.

Stress, circumstances, and failure don't define us if we don't allow them to. Do not let the word "failure" become your identity because something isn't going your way. Drive through it, clear the fog, and find your way.

EXTINGUISHING NEGATIVITY

Become mindful of your negativity. Recognize it and then extinguish it. Suppressing negativity leads to implosion, and so does dwelling in it, thus creating a paradox that can become inescapable. The healthiest way to growth and to continuously move forward is becoming aware. Becoming conscious of everything both positive and negative in your life, but not allowing it to weigh you down. Understand it's there, look at it, tip your hat and say, "good day" and then keep it moving.

Worrying creates poison. It solely attracts negative energy that ultimately is a detriment to your happiness. There's one surefire way to rid negativity from plaguing your mind: do not give power to it. Instead, give flourishing life to positivity, especially in times of distress, no matter how overwhelming things feel. Everything will be, as it should in time. It is imperative that we remain positive when weathering our personal storms because there is only one sure thing about our storms: the sun will surely shine again.

"What you think, you become. What you feel, you attract. What you imagine, you create"

– BUDDUH

QUICK TIP

Have some downtime? Read a book. Find your peaceful place, sit down, and lose yourself for a minute or an hour. Just enjoy it. An idle mind in the presence of stress tends to fuel your negativity. Distract yourself with a great read.

CHAPTER 34

IS YOUR GLASS LOOKING HALF EMPTY?

Fill it up! That's what they always fail to disclose in your choices when asking your perspective on that glass halfway occupied with liquid, don't they? Why is it only half empty or half full? There is a third option to your perspective. The glass is also refillable. You can choose to fill it as you see fit. There is a never-ending abundance of positivity within you to forever keep the glass overflowing at the brim when it appears to be diminishing. Below, there are a few things in mind pertaining to our personal glass:

1. FALSE ADVERTISING

It's tough. It's understandable. It's true. Sometimes our environment, our experiences, our upbringing, and just the way were wired allows us to see the world pessimistically. Life tends to hand us a series of events that seem a lot worse than they are. At face value, everything hard seems impossible. Hardship is real and it's well, hard. We can become caged in a mindset of how everything is that way now and forever because that's how it always has been, just because that's how it was, or how it appears to be now, doesn't define how it's going to be forever. Only you can define what comes next.

2. LOOK OUTSIDE

If it takes you looking at someone else's situation that is worse off to figure out that your glass is actually half full then so be it. You can always have it worse than you do right now. Let that be the spark to the newfound outlook on positivity. The reciprocal is encouraged as well; if it takes the overcoming of hardship in your life to inspire someone else's, then so be it. Everything is "half full" or "half empty," it just depends who's holding the glass.

3. SHARING WITH OTHERS

Fill your glass and then share with others. Be that spark for someone else's positivity, and induce a chain reaction. If you have something positive to say, say it, and if you hold negativity, then snuff it out. It takes so much effort to hate, but in the world today it seems so effortless. Make no mistake, there are far more positive, happy, enthusiastic people in the world, we just have to outshine the darkness. It all starts with that glass you thought was half empty. Walk over to the sink, and fill it up. It's that simple. Now your "half empty glass" is overflowing. So when someone asks you if the glass is half empty or half full, fill it up. Nobody can dispute over a full glass, can they?

CHALLENGE

1. Compliment three people every day, starting the next time you encounter a fellow human.
2. When a half empty perspective arises, remind yourself to say, "It could always be worse."

CHAPTER 35

TRUST THE TIMING OF YOUR LIFE

There are no rules. There's no deadline on how and when your personal milestones should happen. Your current situation is certainly not your final destination. Stress is the only reason why we feel that we have to have everything happen right here and right now. Everything will be as it should and unfold in abundance for you when it is your time, not a second before that. Know yourself, your why, your direction, and the rest will work itself out with the proper mindset and actions. With the right tools, you can build anything.

Every obstacle and set-back wasn't meant to prevent you from your goal, but rather guide you closer to it by showing you what wasn't meant for you and what soon lays ahead. Trust the timing of your life. Make positive progress in the right direction, mindful of your vision, and watch what begins to happen for you. Wholly give yourself over to this notion and find yourself swell with inner peace and feel a calming exhale leave your body along with your stress.

You are not where you are right now by accident. I believe in you and more importantly, you need to believe in you. Nothing is out of your reach. Know that you are meant to travel down a beautiful and wonderful path.

DAILY REMINDERS

1. It's Okay

It's okay that something didn't work out. It's okay to feel behind in life. It's okay to feel everything associated with doubting the process of your personal journey. The important thing is knowing not to make this feeling permanent. Pick yourself back up to keep on going. Breathe. You got this!

2. Don't Waste Energy

Stop wasting energy on things out of your control. Accept your task. Accept your past. Accept your present. Accept that you can't control everything. Place your energy into you next move.

3. Trust Yourself

You are more than capable of creating your ideal life. Trust yourself and the talents you were given. There is nothing handed to you that you are unable to conquer. A powerful enough purpose coupled with your awesomeness will provide everything you need.

4. Gratitude

Be thankful for where you are and everything that has happened leading up until this moment. Learn from your mistakes and be thankful for yet another day to produce effort towards your dreams

CHAPTER 36

HAPPINESS IS...

One of the most intriguing and vague words in all of human language perhaps. Everyone is trying to figure it out as if it's an equation or trying to get there like a destination. What is it? How do you measure it? Who determines it? The answer to every question is inside of you and all around you in your life if you choose it to be.

Some would say it's the feeling provided by the hug of a family member. Some might say it's feeling the sense of pride by personal accomplishments. Some might say it's simply the feeling of security and having a roof over their head. Some may describe it as looking into the eyes of another who means more to them than life itself and having that feeling reciprocated. Children may describe it as finding a prize in the cereal box. Who is anyone to define it other than you? We can all agree that it is, in fact a FEELING. You can't quite describe this feeling as well as you intend to convey, because it is more than words, but you sure can see it radiating from the face of someone who is intimate with it.

LET LOOSE

Not everything has to have an ulterior meaning. Doing something because your heart tossed a lasso around it and started pulling can be exactly what we need at times. If happiness is your goal, then realizing that practicing acts that give you joy is the foundation of your growth. You can plan to be happy, read about being happy, surround yourself with it, but nothing can compare to simple irrational heart indulging happiness that you get from actually DOING what ignites passion.

YOU CAN'T SCHEDULE HAPPINESS

You don't schedule "Happiness: 9:00 to 10:00" into your agenda, so it shouldn't be treated as such in your natural, fluid environment. What you can do is choose long-term goals that require short-term triumphs. Nothing in this world should trump loving your life. Happiness, or anything for that matter just isn't wished for and then granted. It takes a proper mindset, practice, patience, and being mindful of the moments in our life.

"Enjoy the little things, for one day you may look back and realize they were the big things."

– ROBERT BRAULT

Happiness cannot be planned, only experienced. If you're concerned with creating the perfect moment, or waiting for tomorrow, you will undoubtedly ponder in retrospect of the moment you're in right now as a chance to seize what you've been chasing so dearly. Come tomorrow, today will be called yesterday, and with it the moment you spent planning your happiness for today has already passed. It's not too late. The time is now.

HAPPINESS IS A HABIT

Everything we are surrounded by is the consequence of our habits. Happiness is no different. Make it a habit and it shall be your life. We don't always consciously know when we're creating a particular habit until it becomes just that, a habit. Practice this as you would anything you wish to master until it becomes a part of you. "I'm happy" doesn't mean a thing if you don't feel it as the words leave your mouth.

EMBRACE THE FEELING

Everything we do in life comes down to feeling. It's the motivation for most of our actions and choices in situations. For better or worse, we act on emotions, partially and sometimes fully. In our brain, our amygdala plays a part in this by aiding in impulsive decisions with immediate outcomes, but ultimately we make the conscious decision derived from how the outcome will make us feel.

The feeling of the warm sun beaming on your face, the feeling of the rain pelting your skin, the feeling of angst with an upcoming date, the feeling of joy and pride when you've accomplished something; all different senses of the word, but feelings nonetheless. Any robot can complete a task, but it takes a human driven by a feeling to truly be liberated in life to choose his/her path based on what gives them a life worth living.

QUICK TIP FOR A QUICK SMILE

Smile an authentic smile stemming from a positive anchor: a memory, a loved one, a funny movie moment, anything at all. Don't just show your teeth as if you're the only one in sole possession of such a phenomenon though- Smile from ear to ear, a cheek rising, squinty eyed, quintessential poster child for happiness type of smile. Use as needed. Continue with your day.

CHALLENGE

1. Every day: Do something that guarantees your happiness. Form simple habits starting today that you look forward to doing. Maybe it's the gym, a cup of tea by the fire, meditating in the outdoors, find your Zen and dwell in it for even a moment every single day.

2. Right now: do something joyful. Listen to your favorite song, call a loved one, roll up a paper ball at your desk and shoot it into the trashcan as if you just drained the buzzer beater to win the championship. Think of something right now and do it.

CHAPTER 37

UNDERVALUED TIME IN UNEXPECTED PLACES

Every day presents us with opportunities to become mindful in our vision, reflect on ideas, feeling, plans, and anything else you can dream of. This time is hidden between the lines and slips through the cracks of busy everyday life. Found in the most unexpected places, one minute here, five minutes there. The time exists but needs your attention to allow the light to be shed unto. Every single day we are given little pieces of mental gold to unearth. Make sure to cash in! Here are just a few:

SHOWER

The most undervalued time to utilize is your shower time. The shower isn't only for singing. You're distraction free and alone with your thoughts. Use this time for reflection, mapping out your goals for the day, positive affirmations, or meditation. Using this time to refresh and recharge both body and mind is extremely important for what happens next in your day. If you shower at night, apply all of the above for what will happen tomorrow. Make a mental checklist and prepare yourself to dominate your day.

DRIVING

Commuting to work or school is also a great time to do all of the above instead of working up a road rage in traffic imagining that every car in front of you spontaneously combusts. You drive yourself to work and school every day, and you know what to expect, so why stress yourself. The traffic isn't going to change, but your mindset can. Even listening to audiobooks in the car driving or bathroom while showering is a useful way to squeeze in a few minutes of positivity and knowledge into your day. Every minute unused is never coming back, and for those serious about achieving their goals, you know how important this time can be.

LUNCH BREAK

A lunch break is a perfect time to be with yourself, other than to refuel your body, you can use this time as a serious mind recharge as well. Don't squander this opportunity to meditate for a few moments. Take your mind off of the tasks past or ahead and let your mind wander to a place it feels it needs to. Take this time to go over that mental checklist you made in the shower. Are you living today as you said you would yesterday? If not, proceed to do next in the second half of your day what you intended to in the first half.

LAYING IN BED

Before you get out of bed and before you fall asleep use this time to express gratitude for what is about to happen or what has just commenced. It is a gift that you once more open your eyes and then get to lay them to rest at night. Do not let this go unnoticed.

QUICK TIP

From this point forward, become mindful of the time you might be wasting. Every instance you hear yourself saying that you don't have the time, use your unexpected minutes devoted to creating some for yourself or using that undervalued time itself to chip away at what you wish you had more time for.

CHAPTER 38

WRITE A LETTER

One thing that will live on forever is your written word. Take the time to write a letter. In a world of emails, texts, and video chats, the letter has become an endangered species. There is just something so raw, authentic, sensational, personal, and timeless about writing something with a pen flowing ink onto parchment. A piece of who you are, becoming transferred onto paper in your own personal penmanship recreated by none other is a gift unrivaled. The beautiful thing about a letter is that you can't backspace. Whatever thoughts you transcribe must be completed. You can cross it out, but it still wanted to be on that page nonetheless. Don't ignore that. Slow down to the speed of now; let your thoughts and hand flow freely. Try this exercise below for whatever purpose you see fit. Be honest. Be personal. Be raw. Be you.

TO SOMEONE

You can leave your imprint on someone forever by sharing a memory, or even a simple story. That letter can remain alive as long as it has someone to pass down to. Write this letter to anyone of your choosing. Maybe start by telling them why you're writing this letter. Then tell them a story, ask them how they're doing, thank them for being a part of your life, or share a memory in detail as if you were both reliving it. Use the two words, "Remember when…" and let their mind paint the story walking through that moment as if were yesterday. Write anything. Just write it.

It's not about what the letter contains; it's the feeling that it conveys. Your words written in your hand should swell feelings of familiarity, nostalgia, happiness, sadness, love, or anger. The point is to isolate the world around you, and allow the recipient the time to feel significant to you, and for you to recognize this person's significance in your own life.

TO YOURSELF

It could be about anything at all. It can be therapeutic, goal-oriented, or story-oriented. Just try it. Make promises to yourself, set goals to be completed by the time you open it again, share a self-report on your happiness and overall mood that day, speak about your satisfaction in your life, anything. Have a conversation with your future self from this day and describe in detail every single minute of it. Ask yourself questions about where you are now, did anything happen that day to impact where you are now? Throw in things you may be curious to ask your future self.

When you're finished, sign and date it for when you would like to re-open it, or give it to a friend/family member to mail you on that date. A time frame to open it may be six months or six years depending entirely on when you want to read it.

You'll be surprised to see the person who's reading the letter in contrast to the one who wrote it. If you had any plans on personal development in your life then the person who wrote that letter should hopefully sound like a dreamer, a rough draft of the person you are today.

CHAPTER 39

BE HERE NOW

"Sometimes you will never know the value of a moment until it becomes a memory"

– DR. SEUSS

Caught up, looking forward to the next moment and making the next memory. Expecting it to be greater than the unnoticed ones we let unconsciously slip through our fingers like sand, only to remember them as a time we'd give anything to go back to. Be here now and live in what is instead of what will be, for you may never fully understand the value of today until it's gone. You must seize your moments before they depart, unappreciated for what we will come to know what they really meant to you. Make them all count.

LEARNING TO LIVE AROUND YOUR PROBLEMS

Rather than dwelling on your troubles and what weighs you down, learn to live around them. Shift your attention to noticing life, this beautiful life, moment-by-moment that is currently happening right in front of you.

"When every day seems the same, it is because we have stopped noticing the good things that appear in our lives."

– PAULO COELHO

SURRENDER YOURSELF

When you surrender yourself to the moment, you move with ease with every effort flowing with every beat of your heart. Your breath is one with the moment, and it with your breath. Becoming one, moving outward like a free flowing river of power and confidence, here in the moment able to flow freely with the purist intent. Find this moment. Find your Zen.

LIVING IN RETROSPECT

When feeling your body and mind begin to stray from your current experience, take a moment to bring yourself back. Think about today's moments, and what you do will be remembered tomorrow and in the years to come. What are you doing right now? Feel it in your body, feel it in your legs and arms. Take in all of the sensations that your able to harness and feel it all. One day you might be triggered by an anonymous cue to flash you right back to now, remembering it as if you are as present as you currently are.

BE PRESENT WITH...

1. Your Work: Commit your body, mind, and soul to the purpose of your goal. Be there, firing on all cylinders to be as productive and resourceful as you can. Whatever you need to do to position your mind toward productivity, and eliminate distractions, do it. Your results will speak for themselves. Dwell in your flow and ride it to fruition. The most valuable precept is the state of continual awareness.

2. Others: If you're out with friends or on a date, it beckons your full attention. Enjoy it. Soaking in moments as they organically unfold: feeling, listening, reacting, and connecting. Whether you're at a party or watching TV with your partner, that's where you should be. Wholly and completely, allowing not a single stressor to snake its way into the tunnels of your brain. Direct that energy into sharing and attending to the person whom you are with.

3. Yourself: Be in the moment. Never find yourself fretting over thoughts of when and how things will end. When time is idle, your mind drifts into the angst of future events. Brooding about future events that cause you stress, in turn makes you the stressor. Don't become the stress that you fear. It only exists because you are mentally reacting to how you think that moment will feel. Let the feeling and the future moment happen in unison. Set your mind at ease. Ride the wave of the experience that is currently happening. Bask in the elegance of now. Immerse your soul in the beauty of a moment and let tomorrow be tomorrow.

CHAPTER 40

GRATITUDE

The person with the old car wants the new one. The person riding their bike in the rain wishes they had any car at all. The person who walks to work wishes they had that bike; it would save them so much time in the morning. The person in the wheelchair thinks that if they had those legs...they could go anywhere.

Don't be so quick to covet the lives of others in misinterpreted dissatisfaction of your own. The correct interpretation lies not in what you do not have but the failed recognition of what you do have. The dissatisfaction doesn't necessarily dwell in what you possess, but the failure to appreciate it. Appreciation for what we do have makes all the difference. It makes the little seem big, the dull seem shiny, and the worst seem not as bad anymore.

WHEN YOU'RE DOWN, JUST LOOK UP.

There's never a moment to feel ungrateful if you still have a beating heart and air in your lungs. The good, the bad, and the ugly have led us to the second we're in right now and every single moment of it has shaped you into who you are today. That should never go unnoticed. No matter how bad it gets, how hopeless it seems, and how low we can sink...it can always be worse. The most satisfying thought when we're down is looking up since it is the only direction in which to travel.

EVERYTHING HAPPENS *FOR* YOU, NOT TO YOU.

Anything thrown in your path should be accepted with a smile and a thank you. Good or bad, it doesn't matter. As long as you live every day to the best of your abilities, it shapes you to learn and grow. Anything and everything is meant to make you into a better version of yourself. It's a matter of how you receive life. Understanding that life happens for you, not to you is the mindset you must adopt if you wish to become the greatest version of yourself in the pursuit of your vision.

YESTERDAY, TODAY, AND TOMORROW

Here, now, and every day moving forward is the time to be grateful for all that you have gone through, everything you have experienced throughout this year and everything yet to come. It all makes you who you are in this present moment. Be grateful that you made it here (with a few bumps and bruises I'm sure) to yet another day of life. To draw breath down into your lungs, and to experience every sweet and sour taste that life has to offer is a gift in its own. Now is the time to say thank you. Leave behind the worst parts of the past and bring with you the best. Be grateful for it all. Move forward knowing you are better, stronger, and wiser because of it.

QUICK TIP

Every night before going to sleep, think about three positive things that happened throughout your day, even what made you laugh or smile. You might just realize that a bad day was really a good one because there's always someone or something to appreciate within it.

CHALLENGE

1. Write and send a thank you note to every important person in your life, simply thanking him or her for being in it and tell him or her why. It might be just what they needed at just the right time.

2. Write a letter to "Failure and Disappointment." Mention everyone in your life currently or in the past that had a hand in your unhappiness and disappointment. Tell them everything they did and how it made you into the person you are today. From the depths of your soul, feel the pain they caused you and write it in front of you. Write it all. In the end, thank Failure and Disappointment, and their accomplices along the way for bringing you here to where you are right now. Finally, to rub salt in the wound, mention in a postscript, that you are better, stronger, wiser, and happier because of them having stepped into your life. Now rip that letter up. That wasn't for them. It was for you.

CHAPTER 41

IT'S OKAY TO SAY NO

"When you say 'yes' to others, make sure you're not saying 'no' to yourself."

– PAULO COELHO

Just say no. It's okay to be selfish and think of your best interest before the satisfaction of others. If happiness is your goal, then you should do what makes YOU happy. Mind you, the greatest gift can be given and received by becoming selfless and compassionate to the needs of others. That isn't the type of "no" being presented. The one being encouraged is in light of saying a "yes" that spawns a miserable pitted feeling in your gut every time you agree to it. You say yes when you know you should've said no, and now your word vomit has thrust you into another commitment draining your happiness once more. That's the type of "no" you need to say, and the "yes" you want to avoid.

If it is not in the best interest of your overall health, wellbeing, happiness, and you know it, then it's okay to say no. Being a people pleaser is painstakingly difficult to break the habit of, but necessary when tending to the care of your needs first. Here are a few good reasons to say no:

1. Getting in over your head: Saying yes to someone and then being unable to deliver creates a more precarious situation than the one you were in before.

---

2. Adding too much onto your plate: Juggling too many things at one time, and then adding onto that something for someone else will not produce the best results possible. A job done right always trumps efforts that are rushed with little devotion.

3. Builds confidence: It will get easier with every time you say it. Saying no is uncomfortable, but recognizing that your priorities are in the correct order makes things easier.

4. Stop being taken for granted: It provides more value to your YES. People will realize that your time, like all time, is a gift. Someone who chooses to give his or her time wisely will require the other person to take your help seriously. Also, it can help them realize that they can do what they need with the proper resourcefulness. By telling them no, you're helping them find out that they actually can do these things because now they are left absent the choice.

JUST CHOOSE

Choosing your happiness is the same as saying you're going to complete a specific goal. If you don't start now, and take massive action today, then it's most likely you never will. Never put off until tomorrow what you need to do today.

There are luxuries and necessities in this world. What isn't placed at the forefront of our priorities as a necessity, and always should, is our happiness. The time to take back your life and understanding that your decisions are in your full control is now.

Choose happiness. Choose enjoyment. Choose passion. Choose life! All of the above is what we need in our lives, is it not? Becoming mindful that now you must say no in order to say yes for sake of your happiness is all that matters on your path to a radiant and exceptional life.

SECTION FOUR
CONNECT

CHAPTER 42

THE ART OF HUMAN CONNECTION

Empathy is what separates us from everything else on this planet. Our moral integrity is the very foundation of our humanity, and we must hold on to it with every fiber of our being. It is in our nature to be connected. We're wired to connect with each other. We're meant to help each other. We're meant to love each other. We are not here by coincidence coexisting just to ignore one another.

UNDERSTAND TO BE UNDERSTOOD

Before trying a one size fits all approach to a problem or someone's situation, take the time to listen and try to understand what they're feeling with compassion, not only to respond. Understanding exactly what person's feeling is impossible, unless switch bodies with them. The best we can do is understand and offer what we have to give. Empathetic communication is the cornerstone to building authentic, lasting relationships, or simply coming in contact with a human seeking council and conservation.

DON'T LET IT BECOME EXTINCT

Human connection is truly an art form that has faded ever so gently from generation to generation with each and latest technological advancement making communication as brief and impersonal as humanly possible. It's true that art changes and evolves, as does anything else, but the most valuable pieces in the world are the oldest and original. This art form requires open expression and raw emotion, unlike anything that moves to replace it. Technology advances the way in which we communicate, making things more efficient than ever imaginable, while being able to reach someone at the other end of the world with the touch of a button. This in itself is a miracle only dreamed of not long ago. But we also mustn't lose touch with the intimate connection between us out there in the world, beyond the screen, in front of our nose.

"Human beings are like that. We want to live by each other's happiness – not by each other's misery. We don't want to hate and despise one another. In this world there is room for everyone. And the good earth is rich and can provide for everyone. The way of life can be free and beautiful, but we have lost the way."

– CHARLIE CHAPIN

We've since begun to slowly trade in beautiful masterpieces such as sharing a story with a stranger or a common hello accompanied with a smile. Look up once in a while, or you might miss the subtleties in the connection shared within the eyes of another; a laugh shared over a moment with a familiar stranger. We're not so different you and I. Our souls can recognize its counterpoint in another if we let it. Don't miss out on something as miraculous as this. These paintings could fill a gallery, and they would be tagged priceless.

MAKING AN IMPACT

The endless connections with another over a common bond, while being from two completely different walks of life, is why we are here. The tiniest impact on someone's day, or the impact they have on yours could make all the difference. We mustn't lose that. People forget names; days, dates, what you wore, what you did, and what you said, but they will never forget how you made them feel.

TALK TO STRANGERS

Whether for a minute or a lifetime, people will come and go. Everyone who passes through your life has now made an impact on it, and in turn is the most microscopic or continental part of it. This cannot be ignored. Isolation and avoidance of human contact is unnatural. Every person we meet is a new opportunity at an intriguing experience of the senses; the way someone speaks, smells, looks, it's all important and connected to a new and unique moment with everyone being different than the one before it. We all have something different to offer each other. As soon as you start understanding that every day we wake is a new chance to make a connection with another human, is the sooner people will be seen as less of a nuisance and more of a gift placed in our path.

QUICK TIP

Have a conversation to pass the time. Conversing with strangers can be beneficial to our emotional health through something called Fleeting Intimacy, which is when brief social encounters provide us with a feeling of emotional resonance and meaning.

DAILY CHALLENGE

Every single day, make direct eye contact with at least three strangers. Smile, and say hello (start a conversation if possible).

CHAPTER 43

THE GREATEST GIFT

It is in our nature to be kind to one another. Embrace it. Experience what it is to be selfless. Kindness is free and when shown to others, is reciprocated in our own happiness. It all starts with you.

YOUR SMILE CAN CHANGE THE WORLD

No matter how different we are, we're all able to connect. A smile can be translated into every language on every continent. One simple curl to the edges of our lips simultaneously, more than not, induces the same in who it is being directed at. Gestures, thoughts, and actions with kind intentions to connect with one another link us all together. We're like that, you see, not so different after all. An open mind and heart to shared experiences and hidden connections bring us to the purpose we're really meant to fulfill: a deep and meaningful connection to others and the reciprocation of it.

DECIDE TO BE KIND

Your decisions in this day matter and have the potential to change the course of your own or someone else's life for the better or worse. A secret such as this should not go untold. Do right by yourself and right by others, and I'm positive you shan't need anything else to get you out of bed in the morning. Wherever your energy takes you, be there. It matters that you place your energy in the right places.

Be mindful of the struggles in your life behind closed doors because others have them as well. Your struggle is not unique. One form or another is felt in every human on earth. You are unaware of what battles others are fighting in their lives. Therefore, consistently and nonspecifically be kind because it could make all the difference. Since someone wasn't kind to you doesn't mean that you need to pay that forward. Let that person's negativity end there, instead of passing through you, giving it energy to negatively affect someone else's life. In a world where we are but one of billions, everyone deserves to feel like they matter.

"We but mirror the world. All the tendencies present in the outer world are to be found in the world of our body. If we could change ourselves, the tendencies in the world would also change. As a man changes his own nature, so does the attitude of the world change towards him. This is the divine mystery supreme. A wonderful thing it is and the source of our happiness. We need not wait to see what others do "

– MAHATMA GANDHI

RANDOM ACTS

Being kind doesn't have to be a luxury. It is not an evaporating resource. Giving kindness shouldn't be selective. We have an unlimited supply and every single person deserves a little from you. The more you give the more you receive; kindness tends to work that way. There are no words to express the joy had in both you and the person who's face you bring a smile to. The power you have to impact someone else's life in a positive way is the single most amazing thing you can do with your own. Even taking a minute to simply listen without any intention of response to someone that needs an ear can mean everything. Offering a hug to someone who is visibly upset, your shoulder could bear the weight of his or her world. This can range from a tsunami-sized gesture, trickling all the way down to a raindrop-sized one glancing your forehead. Water is still water, no matter the form.

DAILY CHALLENGES

1. Do something for someone that can do nothing for you in return.
2. Compliment three people.
3. Go to bed knowing you were the cause of someone's smile.

CHAPTER 44

LET IT IN, LET IT OUT

Become raw and honest with your feelings, no matter what they are. Not what you're supposed to feel, what you think you should be feeling, or what's "normal." What you really feel, no matter how contrary to your beliefs, needs to be embraced.

LET IT IN

1. Simply Feel. You can't see it, but you know when you feel it. That is the most fundamental contribution to any connection, human or otherwise, isn't it? How it made you feel. We see, hear, smell and touch a myriad of sensations every day, but without feeling attached they possess no deeper connection than what the physiological definition for that sense is, and that's not how we are wired as human beings. We are connected, all of us to each other and to everything.

2. Take the time to explore your feelings. Connection causes us to feel and the deeper we feel about that connection related to a positive or negative connotation perpetuates how much we care. That care grows deeper into love or hate. Both feelings are strong, and however different they may be, they are nearly the same. Opposite ends of the spectrum, but the furthest extremes, which makes them not so different. Feelings are messy, but what would we be if not attached to them? Take the time to understand what part someone is meant to play in your life; experience what it means that their life path has crossed with yours in this moment. Let your feelings light the way.

LET IT OUT

1. Live your life in color. You take the color and the authenticity out of your life by intentionally desensitizing yourself and repressing your feelings. We often can relate certain colors to emotional states, right? Feeling and expression aren't simply red, blue, black or white. It's like picking out a swatch for the color you will paint your walls. Simply choosing red actually means selecting one of what seems like a thousand shades. By desensitizing, you're creating endless shades of grey, unable to tell the difference. Ringing out the color, numb, lackluster, and hardened we become.

2. You're not "too" anything. We're so afraid of externalizing our feelings, afraid to say too much, feel too deeply, love too much. Our worry is that we become "too..." Too, when attached to a word like the ones above are then labeled as a negative connotation, automatically becoming synonymous with the word "crazy," or something that you should be ashamed of. Not by your own standards, because you're the one who is expressing it. If something is "too" much for someone to handle, then the problem lies with them, not you.

3. Own it. There is nothing wrong with you. If you feel it, express it. Don't suppress it. If you love someone, tell them! If you feel like screaming, scream! If you're happy, smile! Nonverbal communication is just as impactful as its counterpart. If you're troubled, confide in someone. The same goes in the other direction as well: if you're dissatisfied, explain why. If you don't like something, then react. What matters is how you feel and how you choose to express it. Be bold in your identity, in who you are and with how you feel. Take pride in it. There's courage in opening up. It takes a strong fortified soul to strip down to their bare nature allowing themselves to be vulnerable and utterly transparent in the moment of a feeling.

CHAPTER 45

THE MUST-HAVES

As we progress through life, we realize that the quality of things begins to matter more than the quantity. Recognize what's precious in your life. Discovering happiness through experiences, love, memories, and laugher is what impacts our lives the most. These words are all interrelated, so where you find one you will also find the others. See to it that every day is filled with each of those words, and you will find that you have both quality and quantity of everything you could ever need.

LOVE

It's the reason for everything; the profound connection between it all is the bedrock of life itself. It exists in our passions and is expressed in our actions. It's the driving force of our existence and is sometimes unconventional and obtuse, but love nonetheless. The time we have is fleeting and death is guaranteed, so find what you love, hold on to it, and love it/them wholly and completely until your dying day. There is so much wasted energy involved in hate and resistance. Accepting what we cannot change and embracing what grips our heart is where we truly start living. Words mean nothing without a meaning attached to them. You may have not known what love meant until someone came along and showed you. Loving yourself comes first and foremost before loving anyone or anything else. Love yourself for who you really are, inside and out.

MEMORIES

A sunset evokes a sense of nostalgia that no one else can understand, and a song can instantaneously teleport you to that moment, that feeling, that memory linked to it. Create something that lasts a life-time. A memory can be as small or monumental as it needs to be. It's a smell, a sight, a moment, a sound; it's anything that connects the present moment to a past one that sticks with us for eternity.

A memory can be a place you go in time of hardship and remind you that life is precious and today will too pass. Think back for a second to the best day you've ever had in your life. Would you trade your car for it? Would you trade you watches and shoes to relive it? You know you would trade any THING for it. Things hold value, but there's nothing more valuable than something that imprints itself into your soul, that's priceless.

LAUGHTER

Laugh every single day. It's one of the most mood-enhancing, en-dorphin-releasing, self-help you can ever find at the expense of zero dollars. You hear it all the time: enjoy your life. But are you really? Not everything is as serious as we make it out to be. In addition to redu-cing the production of stress hormones, laughter has the power to mend the deepest wounds, crumble the sturdiest emotional walls and shine a light piercing your days' darkest clouds. Sometimes we fail to recognize the importance of small and simple things that end up making the biggest differences in our lives. Laughter is one of them. So do yourself a favor and lighten up!

Remember! Life is all about the intangibles; a laugh, a smile, a memo-ry. Laugh often, smile more, and create memories with the ones you love, these are truly the greatest treasures in life. With the help of the intangibles, each day has the potential to be the best you've ever had.

DAILY CHALLENGE
Share a memory and a laugh with someone you love.

CHAPTER 46

BE REAL

A strong sense of awareness paired with actions derived from moral integrity will carry you further in your personal and work relationships than any false sense of identity will. Be real with yourself and let that show in everything that you do. No matter who you are, authenticity shines brighter than the facade of forced connection.

IN YOUR WORK

Your work will never truly be received with a warm welcome if they don't think it's coming from an honest place. Someone doesn't buy into what you do; they buy into why you do it. People aren't stupid. They can sense when you're being unauthentic, and it's the biggest turn off to those on the receiving end in your work and in your life. Staying true to yourself, even down to the way you speak will have inordinately more of an impact on your audience if they know it's real. You're not going to please everyone, but you will attract more people and the right people with authenticity rather than a stage act.

IN YOUR LIFE

It is the same concept only applied to your emotional and overall life satisfaction. When you try too hard and suppress your true self to please others, or be someone you're not, it's the fastest way to a life of regret. If we begin to act contrary to our nature, we feel it churning in our stomachs like our bodies are saying, "what the hell are you doing?"

Just like finding your niche, your personality will connect with others no matter what. It's as simple as this: Real attracts Real. If you proceed through life pretending, don't be surprised when you have nobody there for you when you really need it. Authentic self attracts authentic people, lasting people; people who will be in your life for years to come. This is the basis of establishing a real connection with anyone and anything. Your realness will project outward and work like a magnet drawing what you desire inward.

REMEMBER

Even if you don't see it yourself, others can see the greatness in you and that's the raw truth. Think about funerals. Every single person who speaks says something good about the person regardless if they were shitty on the surface and even below it. Similar to an iceberg, there is something inside all of us that resonates with others although it may be difficult to see. Understand what sets you apart and let that perpetually shine. If you've ever felt left out, ordinary, or less than, I firmly stress to you right now that you are included. You are extraordinary. Be you. Be real.

CHAPTER 47

RELATIONSHIPS

Whether it is romantic, social, or business, there is only one thing to remember. Relationships only travel in one of two directions: You either grow together or you grow apart.

THE BASICS

1. If you're not ready to work then don't apply for the job. You must be fully prepared to fulfill the desires and needs of someone else, being just as important as your own.

2. Effort isn't forfeited once a connection is made. It is not about convenience. It's about being there, sharing, compromise, and making the time to give that person what they need.

3. Ask yourself the right question. It's not, "what am I going to get out of this?" It's, "what am I prepared to give?"

GROWING TOGETHER

When entering a relationship, you're essentially taking two different people from two different lives, two different upbringings, two different personalities, and different perspectives on life, and agreeing to grow together towards a common goal. No two people see a painting the same way; one says they see the ocean as midnight blue while the other sees sapphire. Each of our lives brings contrasting perspectives into a moment's existence as we encounter it. No matter how similar on the surface, disagreements are natural and the compromise in working towards a solution is crucial in the growth of any type of flourishing relationship. Conflict is the greatest opportunity to turn that moment into an opportunity to grow more intimate. Much like personal growth, it is about discovery of what it takes to evolve into the best version rather than the destruction of it.

GROWING APART

Drifting apart is easy, as well as anything that takes little effort and care, but like all things we strive for, you do not wish to see it fail. Your time and energy is too important to be displaced. Anything of worth takes much more of yourself being given, than what you expect to get out of it. A relationship between two people requires hard work. Growing in opposite directions is as simple to spot as it is for it to happen- your time becomes more valuable in your eyes then making the time for the other person's needs. You just don't care. There is a stale feeling of apathy slowly rotting your foundation until one day it breaks apart. Your conflicts aren't used as opportunities to grow as much as they are a battleground to unleash your arsenal of emotional assaults.

ROUTINE MAINTENANCE

The key to successful relationships is to have an attractive, captivating personality. Building bridges may be easier these days with the help of modern technology, but it doesn't replace the people on both ends. The part where some drop the ball is maintaining those relationships, whether it's a personal relationship or customer base. A city doesn't build a bridge and say, "okay it's done, let's never come back." There's work done to ensure it stands the test of time, or else it will crumble. Our relationships are no different.

SECTION FIVE
LIVE

CHAPTER 48

TIME

"Time is too slow for those who wait, too swift for those who fear, too long for those who grieve, too short for those who rejoice, but for those who love, time is eternity."

– HENRY VAN DYKE

One of the few things we have no dominion over. Cry, beg, wish, and dream for more, but it falls upon deaf ears. It keeps moving whether it's in our favor or not. It can be cruel that way. But if we do not squander it, and realize it for what it is then our perception of it also changes. Time is a gift.

USE IT HONESTLY

Whatever is left for you, it's your absolute duty to use it as fully and as honestly as humanly possible. Honestly defined here as: never apologize for the time you use spent on your desires. Do something with as much passion and fire that burns deep within and use your time to surround yourself with it for as long as it lasts. Have you ever danced in your room alone? Have you ever sung your lungs out in the shower? Have you shamelessly indulged in a guilty pleasure when no one was around to speculate? (If you said no you're lying). Do anything that resembles that feeling; careless, spontaneous, joyous, and fulfilling. Spending time on the negative thoughts of yourself and others is time wasted.

TIME ONLY MOVES IN ONE DIRECTION

Don't dwell on the past and things you cannot change. Stop thinking and start doing. Never be idle, always find yourself moving forward because time doesn't wait for anyone.

You've come to this point and make the decisions you did for specific reasons, and that is not wasted time. That is time used wisely in the moment of making a decision is better than not making any decisions at all. The things you chose to do that are written in the chapters in the book of your life was made because of important determining factors that influenced you most at the time of action. The only circumstance that decides whether our time has been wasted or not is if you have learned from your bad decisions, enjoyed the good ones, and have made peace with every one that you have made up to this very second.

Nobody can tell you if your time was misspent, because it's used and goes on influencing the present moment with each fleeting moment. Giving your time is the greatest gift to give to anyone. With an encouraging and enthusiastic heart, go fourth, do whatever fills you with emotion and experience. Make sure spend it with whomever makes you feel alive.

CHAPTER 49

NOTHING GOLD CAN STAY

The sun falls each day to darkness, a reminder that time is fleeting and as fast as the night will pass, so shall the day. Nothing lasts forever; as gloomy as it may be to ponder, the only thing certain in life is death. Everything else in between is fluid and ever-changing. The only gold that really shines once we're gone is the impressions we leave on others; a memory, love, a feeling. These things will last longer than anything money can buy, and the impact left on us by others will last if even if you lose touch. In time memories can fade, and the only thing left remaining is a feeling pressed into your heart to remind us that wherever we go, our feelings will follow. Remember death is inevitable, but what happens until then can shine brighter than anything our imagination can fathom.

You see it all the time, accidental deaths, and the early demise of those taken too soon. In our own lives we've all said to ourselves at least once, "I thought I had more time," with someone or something until it was gone. This shows you how beautiful life can be because of the instant it can be ended in. Living like there's no tomorrow is a common reflective phrase, but have you thought about it in the sense of you living today as if your loved ones had no tomorrow?

Make time for those whom you love. Time is not wasted if it is shared in loving company. Whether it's a minute or an hour, take the time to talk to the important people in your life in case tomorrow you're not able to. There's always a million things you wish you said or wish you did with a loved one once they are with us no longer, but why didn't you do or say at least one of them while they were? There is no right answer or excuse for that question. If you love someone, then you will find a way.

In other instances, connection may have been lost for whatever reason, but I assure you if it is a connection bonded with love, it will always find its way back. Your time, your desires, and those of the ones you love are just as important, and sharing them together is priceless. Never forget that. Do not live life with your loved ones according to time. Live according to moments and the ones you create with them. Time is something we have no control over or a countdown to when it ends for any of us. Make the time. Find your gold. Nothing lasts forever.

CHAPTER 50

FLIP THE HOURGLASS ON THREE. ONE, TWO...

Imagine you've just been told the date of your death. Flip the hourglass on three: one... two... three. Now what? You know exactly the time you have left. What are you about to do with it?

What if we counted our lives backwards instead of forward? What if we counted down the years left instead of years lived? You would certainly be living more vigorously and with a sense of urgency, right? Who says we can't live that way from this point on?

Technically, we are counting down. We just don't know when our time is up. The idea of knowing when you expire makes you want to live for what you really want, and include what really matters most. The crazier question to ask ourselves is why aren't we doing it?

REFLECTIVE EXERCISE

Stop, close your eyes, and reflect on the answer after every question:

- You suddenly knew that you had one minute to live. What would you do?
- That minute just turned into an hour, now what?
- That hour just tuned into a day, and so forth, what then? What would you do starting tomorrow?
- Where would you go? What would you change?

- Who would you surround yourself with?
- Are you getting mental pictures, feelings, and who is included in all of these answers?
- If none of that sounds familiar to your current life, why not? The question still remains, why aren't you doing any of it?

START LIVING TODAY

We have so little of it, and waste so much of it doing things we hate. Too many of us are tricking ourselves into believing were living a life that we always wanted for ourselves, but it's not. The good news is that it isn't too late. Start living now! Remind yourself often, as morbid as it sounds, that every day you are counting down instead of counting up.

Stop doing things you hate and start doing things that light up your eyes, that wrenches a smile into your face no matter how low you are. Own your responsibilities and live passionately in unison with them. Create a life you can love everyday instead of enjoying it where the spare time allows you to. Rome wasn't built in a day and neither is the life you're dreaming of. The person with too much structure might want for less and the person with none will yearn for more. There's no such thing as the perfect lifestyle, only the perfect lifestyle for you. The goal is to design the life that inspires effortless happiness and a warm feeling of content. It takes tiny, positive efforts each and every minute. If you're alive, then it's possible. Time is ticking. What's your next move?

CHAPTER 51

YOU WILL DIE, BUT WILL YOU LIVE?

It's not necessarily death that were afraid of or death that inspires us to live. It's that each day you approach it and then finally do, you finally realize you never really lived. That's what is scary. The most dangerous word to humanity in human literacy is regret.

LIFE IS SHORT

Ask the person who was just diagnosed with terminal cancer. Ask the parent that lost a child. Ask anyone who knows they are close to their last breath. Ask the person who walked so close to death that they know the touch of its icy hand on their shoulder. In the context of how healthy you may be today, it seems as if life may never end, but understanding even in our healthiest moments the phrase, "Life is Short" is as true as water is wet. Think about your age today and how fast it crept up on you from the feeling that just yesterday you were leaning how to ride a bike. So I implore you to live! Live not in fear of death, but in fear of regret. Live with ferocity. Live with passion. Live to love. Live to enjoy. Live to feel. Just Live. Stop worrying so much about what you did yesterday or what you will do tomorrow and start living for today.

REMINDER

When sparked with desire, ask yourself, why not? If you don't have a good enough answer that circles around life or death, then roll the dice. Odds are, the fact that you want to do it in the first place means that you'll be happy to know at least you did it no matter the outcome.

Instead of lying in bed that night angry with yourself for not being brave enough to even try.

IN THE END

It's not about what you did it's what you didn't do. It's every winking moment you weren't doing things you wanted to. It's the risks you were too afraid to take, and the dreams you failed to chase. It's the things that you don't do that will haunt you with every living breath until your last. If you want it, go get it. If you dream it, do it. If you're tempted, try it. It's not about winning or losing and it's not pass or fail. It's quite simply live or die.

All of us die; it's just how we go about getting there. Don't regret anything. Never regret anything. Everything we do, we do for a reason. The reason is up to you, but never regret the things you do, just learn from them. Life is less about reaching a destination, and rather more about learning and growing. Every failure is a lesson and every success is growth. Do everything, do anything, just don't find yourself regretting doing nothing.

"Imagine if you will being on your death bed – And standing around your bed – the ghosts of the ideas, the dreams, the abilities, the talents given to you by life. And that you for whatever reason, you never acted on those ideas, you never pursued that dream, you never used those talents, we never saw your leadership, you never used your voice, you never wrote that book. And there they are standing around your bed looking at you with large angry eyes saying we came to you, and only you could have given us life! Now we must die with you forever. The question is – if you die today what ideas, what dreams, what abilities, what talents, what gifts, would die with you? "

– LES BROWN

Don't allow yourself to start a single sentence from this moment forward with "I wish I would have..." Eliminate the word 'wish' from your future vocabulary. Let it be that today you live for what you wish to do tomorrow, instead of what you didn't do yesterday. Don't wish for it. Create it! Live until regret becomes merely a word you know the meaning of, not a feeling you're familiar with.

IT'S ALL ABOUT WHAT YOU DO IN THE DASH

"To live is the rarest thing in the world.
Most of us just exist."

– OSCAR WILDE

A gravestone has two dates on it "born on - died on" that little dash in the middle of those two dates is the only thing that matters more than the day you were born. That little dash represents every single day after you were gifted with your first breath until your last. It represents everything you are, were, and will be through your legacy. What will you choose to do with your dash? What stories will that dash tell? What legacy will you have created? Will it represent a life lived truly, happily, daringly, passionately, and beautifully, or will it just prove that you existed?

Ask yourself, will I live or will I just exist?

JUST A THOUGHT
THE END

CHAPTER 52

AFTERWORD FROM THE AUTHOR

Thank you!

From the bottom of my heart I appreciate you. I'm gracious for every second of your time spent here with me. My one and only goal in writing this is to positively impact you and evoke feeling and thought. To have at least one sentence between these covers that speaks to you as deeply as you do to yourself. If I have, then my mission is complete. Read it again, refer it to another, use what you need, and discard the rest. The choice is yours. I am just grateful for being able to connect with you at all. My name is Dave, and it is my utmost pleasure to meet you. Do not hesitate to find and contact me with any questions, comments, concerns, or simply to say, hey.

Now, thank yourself! Thank yourself for understanding that wanting more doesn't mean that you're less than amazing, only that you know how valuable your life is and what you want is exactly what you deserve. Thank yourself for seeking to grow and develop the greatness you are meant for, inside and out.

This book can be read in any direction, starting from the last page to the first and vice versa. No matter what page you start or end with, the message is the same: You create your life from the inside out.

This book is cyclical, not linear. There is no beginning or end, only now. Success, happiness, connection, and everything in between are within your reach. All begins inside, moves outward, and then returns in abundance, as would a boomerang.

Go now. Whatever you're searching for, I know you'll achieve it. Go write your story. Go create memories. Go laugh, love, experience every sensation. Go feel, express, connect, succeed, and be happy! Create the life you deserve, which is nothing short of something beautiful. Most importantly, just go live. Don't take my word for it. In the end, it's all... just a thought.

With love,

David A. Volpe